PAUL'S USE OF THE OLD TESTAMENT
IN THE EPISTLE TO THE ROMANS

AN ANALYSIS AND COMMENTARY

GREGORY J. NEEDHAM

"Scripture quotations taken from the (NASB®) New American Standard Bible®, Copyright © 1960, 1971, 1977, 1995 by The Lockman Foundation. Used by permission. All rights reserved. www.lockman.org"

Copyright © 2021 by Gregory J. Needham
Publisher: Biblical Understanding

All rights reserved. No part of this book may be reproduced, scanned, or distributed in any printed or electronic form without permission.
First Edition: June 2021
Printed in the United States of America
ISBN: 978-0-578-92995-8

DEDICATED TO
MY WIFE BARBARA

CONTENTS

	INTRODUCTION
CHAPTER 1	THE IMPORTANCE OF PAUL'S GOSPEL ROMANS CHAPTER 1 1:17
CHAPTER 2	NEED OF THE RIGHTEOUSNESS OF GOD ROMANS CHAPTER 2 2:6...2:24
CHAPTER 3	CONDEMNATION OF ALL MEN ROMANS CHAPTER 3 3:4...3:10-12...3:13...3:14...3:15-17...3:18
CHAPTER 4	ILLUSTRATION OF JUSTIFICATION FROM THE OLD TESTAMENT ROMANS CHAPTER 4 4:3...4:7-8...4:9...4:17...4:18...4:22
CHAPTER 5	BELIEVER'S PRACTICE IN REGARDS TO THE LAW ROMANS CHAPTER 7 7:7
CHAPTER 6	BRUTE FORCE DOES NOT NULLIFY THE PLAN OF GOD ROMANS CHAPTER 8 8:36
CHAPTER 7	ELECTION AS EXPLANATION OF ISRAEL'S UNBELIEF ROMANS CHAPTER 9 9:7...9:9...9:12...9:13...9:15...9:17 9:25...9:26...9:27...9:28...9:29...9:33
CHAPTER 8	REJECTION OF ISRAEL ROMANS CHAPTER 10 10:6...10:7...10:8...10:11...10:13...10:15 10:16...10:18...10:19...10:20...10:21
CHAPTER 9	RESTORATION OF ISRAEL ROMANS CHAPTER 11 11:3...11:4...11:8...11:9-10 11:26...11:27...11:34...11:35

CHAPTER 10	RIGHTEOUSNESS OF GOD IN BELIEVER'S LIVES ROMANS CHAPTER 12-15 12:19...12:20...13:9...14:11...15:3 15:9...15:10...15:11...15:12...15:21
CONCLUSION	
APPENDIX I	OUTLINE: PAUL'S EPISTLE TO THE ROMANS
APPENDIX II	LXX TO MASORETIC TEXT TO PSALM NUMBERING
APPENDIX III	CROSS REFERENCE
APPENDIX IV	ABBREVIATIONS
BIBLIOGRAPHY	

Introduction

The interest for this analysis and commentary comes from Biblical hermeneutics. The method used is based on an historical grammatical method of Bible study. The overriding theme for the entire Bible is what Jesus has told us, it is all about Him, "Then beginning with Moses and with all the prophets, He explained to them the things concerning Himself in all the Scriptures." (Luke 24:27)

The intent of this study is not to comment on the Roman Epistle verse by verse, but to address the sections where the Apostle cites the Old Testament as reference.

The Christ centered introduction that Paul writes of in Romans 1:2, referencing the gospel promise coming "through His prophets in the Holy Scriptures" does not limit his Old Testament use to just the prophets, the references show that he considers all the Old Testament as the Word of God.

There is an outline of the Roman Epistle in the Appendix I for reference and continuity. It will be helpful if the reader can read Greek and Hebrew or can access an interlinear Bible in hard copy or on the internet, for their own edification. The Scriptures are for all to understand and believe. Esoteric theological excursions only take away from a common sense approach to explain the passages and are intended to be avoided. The Bereans (Acts 17:10-11) are models of the approach that should be taken when hearing Biblical teaching, "examining the Scriptures daily *to see* whether these things were so."

In the Roman Epistle, the phrase "as it is has been written" (καθὼς γέγραπται), is used by Paul 14 times and "for it has been written" (γέγραπται γάρ) 2 times in the epistle. Not every instance of an Old Testament citation is from the Hebrew Old Testament (MT). Many times, he cites from the LXX (Septuagint). This puts a positive context on the reliability of the LXX translation. It is the Word of God for Paul (2 Peter 1:21), and anyone else who reads it, at least in the sections he cites.

Significant is the καθὼς γέγραπται in Romans 1:17, as Fritz Rienecker notes:

The perfect emphasizes the permanent and authoritative character of that which was written.[1]

Commenting of the second occurrence of καθὼς γέγραπται (Romans 2:24), using the Old Testament as authoritative and as the Word of God, James Denney points out:

What the closing of the sentence with καθὼς γέγραπται suggests is not that it occurred to Paul after he had finished that he had almost unconsciously been using Scripture: it is rather that there is a challenge in the words, as if he had said, Let him impugn this who dare contest the Word of God.[2]

In the discussion of γέγραπται (gegraptai) and its uses, the Gottlob Schrenk makes several points regarding the concept.[3]

---

1 Fritz Rienecker, A Linguistic Key to the Greek New Testament Vol. 2. Zondervan Publishing House, 1980, page 2.
2 James Denney, ed., W. Robertson Nicoll, The Expositor's Greek Testament, Vol. II, Wm. B. Eerdmans Publishing Grand Rapids, Michigan, reprinted 1979, page 600.
3 Gottlob Schrenk, ed. Gerhard Kittel, trans. Geoffrey Bromiley, (TDNT) Theological Dictionary of the New Testament Vol. I, Wm. B. Eerdmans Publishing Grand Rapids, Michigan, reprinted 1979 10th printing 1979, pp. 744-747.

1. It is an important mark of revelation.
2. The Old Testament has an authoritative significance.
3. It mediates the declaration of the will of God.
4. καθὼς γέγραπται is used as an confirmatory formula.

The sacred writings the Christian Church accepted today as God's revelation are the same as the Apostle accepted and are authoritative. They are the Words of God and have the final say on matters of the Christian Religion. Not to view the Scriptures in this light, puts one at odds with the sacred writings and the Lord Himself. It is a common attack upon the faith to promote ideas that the Scriptures are some sort of mythological conglomeration, a solely man sourced group of documents. It is also a common error among Christians that the Scriptures are like an encyclopedia, to look up rules to apply, so as to be a good person, a Scripture a day keeps the devil away, or reading it is like taking a spiritual vitamin, even if you don't understand, while missing the context of a passage and the overall context of the entire Bible, God's salvation for mankind. The message gets distorted when one can go to church and listen to a sermon that falls short and misses this point. Currently, there is a winsome attitude prevalent in the pulpits, that fails to press the serious nature of the gospel upon the listeners. The question, if an unbelieving person were to enter a Sunday morning service in any church, would that person understand who Jesus is and why He had to die?

The inference throughout the Scripture is that those that come to the Christian Faith and the message of salvation, also believe that God is the Creator (Romans 1:20, Hebrews 1:1 and 1:10, Mark 13:19, 2 Peter 2:4, Genesis 1:1) and that the Bible teaches *creatio ex nihilo*. Why is it that many that profess the Christian Faith accept the standard evolutionary science and unquestioned in the education systems, inference being that the material universe is eternal?

While the Epistle is written to the Church in Rome, it is Paul's systematic presentation to the universal Christian Church, and states that mankind suppresses this truth (Romans 1:18). If people reject this truth, they are essentially rejecting the authority of Scripture. Paul writes to the Roman Church citing the Old Testament Scriptures authoritatively. Some Christians in the churches today are confused on this point and their thinking has been obfuscated by the counter views explaining existence and the material world.

The question arises as to why men do not believe? It is the result of the fall and the damage done to the race. Paul details this for us in Romans and other epistles. On our own, without the regeneration of the Holy Spirit (Titus 3:5), we can only disbelieve, there is no spiritual good in us. The unregenerate man does not accept spiritual things, i.e., the authority of Scripture (1 Corinthians 2:14-15).

Alvin Baker describes non acceptance of Biblical authority by the natural man:

The fall of man has impacted the *intellect* (2 Corinthians 4:4, Romans 1:28; Ephesians 4:17-18; 1 Corinthians 1:18), the *emotions* (Romans 8:5-8; Romans 1:26; 1 Timothy 4:2; Hebrews 9:14; Titus 1:15) and the *will* (Romans 5:6; Jeremiah 17:5, 13:23; Romans 1:29; James 4:4). Jesus summarizes the state of man apart from regeneration (John 3:19). We simply cannot accept, welcome or judge rightly the Word of God.[4]

There are multiple cases that will be considered in this study to be prophecy, as foretelling future events. The meaning of προφητεία as Joseph Henry Thayer defines:

---

4 Alvin L. Baker, ThD, Systematic Theology, lecture: 'The depravity of man', Northeastern Bible College, Fall 1981.

prophecy i.e., a discourse emanating from divine inspiration and declaring the purposes of God, whether by reproving and admonishing the wicked, or comforting the afflicted, or revealing things hidden; especially by foretelling future events.[5]

Inasmuch as the entire New Testament might be considered fulfillment of prophecy and God's promised fulfillment from the beginning (Genesis 3:15), since it centers on Christ's coming, in this study an analysis of a category of *fulfilled prophecy* that has a specific historical event as an antecedent will be covered (see Appendix III for categories). When the Apostle cites the Old Testament and it is not in the other categorical uses detailed and the foretelling of future is clear in the Apostle's citations, then it will be considered as a *prophecy fulfilled*. As Appendix III indicates some are coupled with other categories. Another aspect to these citations is Romans 14:11 and 12:19-20. These citations continue a prophecy with an eschatological *prophecy,* so Paul makes it a continuing fulfilling *prophecy.*

HISTORICAL PROPHECY AND SETTING	FORETOLD EVENT(S)
HABAKKUK 2:4 *IMPENDING CHALDEAN INVASION*	ROMANS 1:17 *FAITH IN THE GOSPEL*
PSALM 62:12 *DAVID'S PERSECUTION BY ABSALOM*	ROMANS 2:6 *ESCHATOLOGICAL WRATH STORE HOUSING GUARANTEE*
PSALM 51:14 *DAVID'S SIN OF ADULTERY*	ROMANS 3:4 *RECOGNITION OF SIN REVEALS THE MERCY OF GOD AND THE NEED FOR HIS RIGHTEOUSNESS*

---

5 Joseph Henry Thayer, translated revised and enlarged, Greek English-Lexicon of the New Testament, Harper & Brothers, New York, Cincinnati, Chicago, American Book Company, 1889, page 552.

GENESIS 15:6; PSALM 32:1-2
ABRAHAMIC COVENANT (FATHER OF ALL THE FAITHFUL); DAVID'S RECOGNITION OF JUSTIFICATION

ROMANS 4:3,17,18,22
DECLARATION OF JUSTIFICATION BY FAITH

PSALM 44:22
CALL FOR THE LORD'S DELIVERING ISRAEL FROM PERSECUTION

ROMANS 8:36
UNIVERSAL PERSECUTION STARTING WITH APOSTOLIC ERA

HOSEA 2:23; HOSEA 1:10
SYMBOLIC MARRIAGE AND BETROTHAL OF GOD'S PEOPLE

ROMANS 9:25 ROMANS 9:26
CALLING OF THE GENTILES

DEUTERONOMY 30:11-14
PROMISED RESTORATION FROM CAPTIVITY

ROMANS 10:6-7
CHRIST'S ADVENT AND RESURRECTION

ISAIAH 28:16
WARNING AND CONDEMNATION TO EPHRAIM/JERUSALEM

ROMANS 9:33
ROCK OF OFFENSE IS THE ROCK OF SALVATION

ISAIAH 28:16; JOEL 2:32
PROPHECY OF LAST DAYS AND OUTPOURING OF HOLY SPIRIT

ROMANS 10:11;13
UNIVERSAL PROCLAMATION OF THE GOSPEL

ISAIAH 52:7
PROPHECY OF FALL OF BABYLON AND NEWS OF DELIVERANCE

ROMANS 10:15
APOSTOLIC COMMISSION TO THE CHURCH

ISAIAH 53:1
PROPHECY OF ISRAEL IN BONDAGE TO HER ENEMIES WILL BE DELIVERED BY MESSIAH

ROMANS 10:16
APOSTOLIC PREACHING OF THE GOSPEL

DEUTERONOMY 32:21
MOSES NEAR THE END OF HIS LIFE TO

ROMANS 10:16
APOSTOLIC PREACHING OF THE GOSPEL

ALL THE ASSEMBLY: THE SONG OF MOSES; AFTER CROSSING RED SEA AND DESTRUCTION OF PHARAOH

TO THE GENTILES

ISAIAH 29:10; DEUTERONOMY 29:4; PSALM 69:22-23
PROPHECY OF THE INVASION OF JUDEA, DISCIPLINE GIVEN BY GOD; MOSES DECLARATION OF COVENANT IN MOAB; RESULTS OF MESSIANIC REJECTION

ROMANS 11:8-10
THE CONTINUOUS BLINDING OF ISRAEL TO THE GOSPEL

ISAIAH 59:20-21; ISAIAH 27:9
PROMISE OF THE KINSMAN REDEEMER AND DELIVERANCE OF ISRAEL

ROMANS 11:26-27
MYSTERY REVEALED-POST FULLNESS OF THE GENTILES, ALL ISRAEL WILL BE SAVED

PROVERBS 20:22; 25:21-22
WISDOM GIVEN FOR LIFE AND CONDUCT

ROMANS 12:19-20
PROMISE OF GOD'S ESCHATOLOGICAL JUDGMENT AND CURRENT PRACTICAL DEPORTMENT FOR THE BELIEVER THAT MIGHT BRING ENEMIES TO REPENTANCE

ISAIAH 45:23
DECLARATION OF GOD'S SUPREME POWER

ROMANS 14:11
PROMISE OF ESCHATOLOGICAL JUDGMENT SEAT OF GOD WHERE ALL WILL BE JUDGED

PSALM 69:9
MESSIANIC PSALM AND LAMENT FOR PERSONAL DELIVERANCE FROM STATE OF FORSAKENNESS

ROMANS 15:3
VICARIOUS ATONEMENT OF CHRIST IS THE CHRISTIAN'S MODEL OF FORBEARANCE

PSALM 18:49 OR 2 SAMUEL 22:50
DEUTERONOMY 32:43
PSALM 117:1
ISAIAH 11:10
HISTORIC RECORD ITERATES THE PROPHECY OF THE GENTILE BELIEF AND REASON TO REJOICE WITH ISRAEL; SONG OF MOSES SAID THE SAME; PSALMIST GIVING GLORY TO GOD FOR

ROMANS 15:9
ROMANS 15:10
ROMANS 15:11
ROMANS 15:12
GENTILES ARE REMINDED OF CHRIST'S SERVITUDE TO THEM AND RECIPIENTS OF GOD'S MERCY, THEREFORE ACCEPT ONE ANOTHER

THIS PROPHETIC EVENT;
PROLEPTIC SPEAKING OF CHRIST'S
RETURN AND THE REGENERATION

ISAIAH 52:15 ROMANS 15:21
PROPHECY OF THE UNIVERSAL *PAUL'S ASPIRATION TO PREACH THE*
PROCLAMATION OF THE GOSPEL *GOSPEL WHERE IT HAS NOT BEEN HEARD*

The question, how does the Old Testament *prophetical* words that Paul references have a dual immediate historical foretelling and later completion? In accord with Luke 24:37, 2 Peter 1:19-21 and 2 Timothy 3:16-17, the entire Bible is simply not a human product. To be sure an unregenerate man (Psalm 10:4) will ignore and the atheist (Psalm 14:1) will scoff at this assertion. (cf. 2 Corinthians 4:4).

J. Barton Payne sheds light on this observation commenting on Isaiah's prophecy concerning Immanuel:

The Messiah would then Himself replace once and for all the merely human Jewish kings of Ahaz' house and character. Isaiah's prophecy, furthermore, showed no inaccuracy when it predicted that Ahaz' enemies would be destroyed "before the child knew how to refuse evil and choose the good"; Immanuel did not, in fact, appear for over seven centuries! But this extended lapse of time does not diminish the contemporary relevance of Isaiah's threat. On the principle of "prophetic telescoping," the prophets not infrequently described, as if in an immediate succession, events that later proved to be separated by even millennia (cf. Isa. 11:1-6; 62:1, 2.).[6]

Paul the Apostle and Older Testament expert and New Testament prophet (1 Thessalonians 4:16; 1 Corinthians 13:12;

---

6 J. Barton Payne, The Theology of the Older Testament, Zondervan Publishing House, Grand Rapids, Michigan, 1962, 11th printing 1978, page 269.

15:14), naturally reads the Scripture as an integrated, Divine originated record of God's redemptive plan that reveals over centuries and still is to come and can reference the prophets in this manner.

CHAPTER 1

THE IMPORTANCE OF PAUL'S GOSPEL

BECAUSE IT REVEALS THE RIGHTEOUSNESS OF GOD
THE PROPHECY OF HABAKKUK
1:17   HABAKKUK 2:4

In chapter 1, there is one citation to the Old Testament. Paul is giving the reason how his gospel reveals the righteousness of God. Romans 1:17, "For in it *the* righteousness of God is revealed from faith to faith; as it is written, "BUT THE RIGHTEOUS *man* SHALL LIVE BY FAITH." The reference is from Habakkuk 2:4, "Behold, as for the proud one, His soul is not right within him; But the righteous will live by his faith.", a direct quote from part of the Prophet's writing, the opposition of the just and the unjust.

The LXX says "the just shall live by my faith". The adherence to faith in God and the prophet as the spokesman for Him. The LXX translation uses "my", meaning reference to God given faith, and parallel to the Hebrew "his", God speaking, as the source. Paul also drops the MT "his". God being the owner and giver of faith. The God given faith saves from the wrath of God for all that believe.

Albert Barnes puts it this way:

The Septuagint translate the passage in Habakkuk, 'If any man shall drawback, my soul shall have no pleasure in him, but the just by my faith," or by faith in me, "shall live." The very words are used by them which are employed by the apostle, except they add the word "my," mou, MY faith. The Syriac renders it in a similar manner, "The just by faith shall live." The meaning of the Hebrew in Habakkuk is the same.

It does not refer originally to the doctrine of justification by faith; but its meaning is this, "The just man, or the righteous man, shall live by his confidence in God."[7]

Frederic Godet in a similar manner explains 'my' this way:

In the Hebrew it is: *his* faith (*emouthano*); but the LXX have translated as if they had found *eniounathi*, my faith (that of God), which might signify either my *faithfulness* or faith *in me*. What the translators thought is of small importance. Paul evidently goes back to the original text, and quotes exactly when he says: *"his* faith," the faith *of* the believer in his God.[8]

James Denney summarizes Paul's assertion for man's need for God's righteousness:

The broad sense seems to be that in the revelation of God's righteousness for man's salvation everything is of faith from first to last. *Cf.* 2 Corinthians 2:16; 2 Corinthians 3:18. This N.T. doctrine the Apostle finds announced before in Habakkuk 2:14. ἐκ πίστεως in the quotation is probably to be construed with ζήσεται. To take it with δίκαιος (he who is righteous by faith) would imply a contrast to another mode of being righteous (*viz.*, by works) which there is nothing in the text to suggest. The righteous who trusted in Jehovah were brought by that trust safe through the impending judgment in Habakkuk's time; and as the subjective side of religion, the attitude of the soul to God, never varies, it is the same trust which is the condition of salvation still.[9]

---

7 Albert Barnes, Barnes' Notes on the Bible, Volume 13 - Acts – Romans, AGES Software Rio, WI USA Version 1.0 © 2000, comment on Romans 1:17, page 709.
8 Frederic Godet St Paul's Epistle to the Roman Theological Library.,trans. A. Cusin, new series., Vol. II, Edinburgh: T & T Clark, 38 George Street. 1881, page 162.
9 James Denney, ed. W. Robertson Nicoll, The Expositor's Greek Testament, Vol. II, Wm. B. Eerdmans Publishing Grand Rapids, Michigan, reprinted 1979, page 591.

Karl Keil and Franz Delitzsch assert this about Habakkuk's citation:

There is no question that Paul declares the doctrine of justification by faith alone, "The deep meaning of these words has been first fully brought out by the Apostle Paul (Romans 1:17; Gal 3:11: see also Hebrews 10:38), who omits the erroneous μου of the LXX, and makes the declaration ο δίκαιος εκ πίστεως ζήσεται the basis of the New Testament doctrine of justification by faith."[10]

Heinrich Meyer states that it is clearly prophetic:

This, as the Messianic sense intended to be conveyed by the Spirit of God (2 Peter 1:21) in the prophetic words, Habakkuk 2:4, "the righteous shall by his faithfulness live" (attain the theocratic life-blessedness), is recognised by Paul, and expressed substantially in the language of the LXX., rightly omitting the μου, which they inaccurately add to πίστεως.[11]

This is a fulfilled *prophecy*. It is a communication from God through the prophet to mankind. He addresses the recipients of his epistle in Romans 1:8 "First, I thank my God through Jesus Christ for you all, because your faith is being proclaimed throughout the whole world.", evidence the prophecy is being continually fulfilled, then and now when people believe the gospel which is God's standing command for all men. (Mark 1:15; Acts 2:38; 3:19; 8:22; 17:30; 26:30)

---

10 C. F. Keil & F. Delitzsch, trans. James Martin, Commentary on the Old Testament Vol. 10: Minor Prophets, Wm. B. Eerdmans Publishing Grand Rapids, Michigan, reprinted 1982, page 74.
11 H. A. W. Meyer's, Critical and Exegetical Commentary on the New Testament, Romans, Vol. V., Alpha Greek Library, Winona Lake Wisconsin, reprinted 1980, page 53.

As the world measures things, this is not spectacular. In many churches, particularly some of the large television ministries, this is mundane and ignored, not exciting, not personal wealth building and not self empowering to command the direction of your life. Many examples can be found by just watching Sunday morning television. Some of these preachers have offered step by step mini-projects for the listener's weekly self-improvement lists, even suggesting diets, weight loss methods and financial prosperity plans.

This can all be done because you are empowered. There is seldom any talk of our current state, or the fact that we are sin. Martin Luther's concept "Simul justus et peccator, at the same time righteous and a sinner", explains the dilemma of the Christian.[12]

Much of the state of the contemporary American Christian Church can be capsulized in understanding the Theology of Glory and the Theology of the Cross.

William Graham Tullian Tchividjian's opinion article in The Christian Post addresses this issue. He goes on to say that Jesus is presented as the answer to all of one's problems. He also makes several points on this topic:[13]

1. It is primarily about personal improvement.
2 Accepting Jesus as your Lord and Savior, will make all your dreams come true.
3. Theology of glory and the theology of the cross did not

---

12 Martin Luther, Luther's Works, Hilton C. Oswald ed., Vol. 25, Lectures On Romans, Concordia Publishing House, St. Louis, Missouri, 1972, page 258. Luther's explanation of Romans 4:7.
13 William Graham Tullian Tchividjian, excerpts from 'Theology of Glory vs. Theology of the Cross'. The Christian Post, July 12, 2012, www.christianpost.com/news/theology-of-glory-vs-theology-of-the-cross.html (HTML download on 2/18/2021).

originate with Luther, he just named them, they are old concepts.
4. The theology of glory is the default value because it gives us control. It denies our sinfulness and God as transformer.
5. A theology of the cross, in contrast, does not deny the pain, suffering and wreckage of out lives and sees God at work in these things.
6. Theology of glory will always consider grace as something of a supplement to whatever is left out, from human will and power.
7. With the theology of glory, life is like a ladder we climb scoring victories and points like on a scorecard.

Paul addresses the conflict of two natures the Christian lives with (Romans 7:14-25). Although, we receive a taste of what is to come (Romans 8; 1 Corinthians 2:9), we are not there yet and we don't get it all now. Part of the marketing for some of Sunday morning religious television promotes a popular view that lives under the delusion that the Word of God is some sort of talisman to grant your current desires. As inferred, if these steps are taken and these principles followed, health, wealth and success will result. This criticism by no means diminishes the benefits of the wisdom and didactic portions of the Scripture that guide us, as in the *third use of the Law* (2 Corinthians 9:7-8).

The Biblical model for the Christian starts with the Savior. Jesus wasn't wealthy, Matthew 8:20 and Luke 9:58, Jesus said to him, "The foxes have holes and the birds of the air *have* nests, but the Son of Man has nowhere to lay His head." Paul's life would fail to meet these standards (2 Corinthians 11:24-27). This popular message is nothing more than the concept positive thinking recycled and bereft of the saving explicit of the Christian Faith and its eschatological fulfillment. Sometimes implied in these messages are promises that all one's problems will be solved. This should not be readily believed, because Jesus cautions the opposite i.e., having tribulation in this world (John 16:33). There is a fatigue that comes from listening to and observing pastor cults that promise the absence of tribulation that Jesus speaks of.

The pronoun 'I' is the most frequently used pronoun in these sermons that promise an unfounded Biblical experience. It is sometimes inferred by these pastors, that they have a special relationship with God. Stories are heard of the pastor recounting how a friend was miraculously healed, because that is how the doctors explained the recovery, making a miracle synonymous with God's wisdom and goodness expressed in providential care and guidance (Psalm 36:6-7; 145:9; 1 Timothy. 4:8; Romans 8:28). To reinforce the special status of the pastor, some of these pastors make statements like "God told me to buy a blue car". The congregants know they are not hearing this sort of communication from God and are somehow inferior spiritual Christians. The next question is do these pastors actually claim or think they hear an audible voice and then assume it must be God's voice?

One experience recounts how a church held a revival week, inviting a special designated evangelist from the denominational affiliation. If one was in attendance they would have been puzzled to hear this evangelist who made the preface to the sermon "when I woke at 6 AM, the Lord gave me this sermon." Allowing for metaphorical speech, this meeting was on Saturday at 10 AM. It was quite clear, after listening to the sermon, this could not be true, unless you believe the God of the Scriptures engages in low quality entertainment by his servants and that ministers do not have to prepare diligently for sermons. No doubt that this standard ruse was being used to engrandize the preacher's status and to make the hearer think that they do not have his spiritual elevated position. Decide for yourself, have you have ever experienced this?

Hearing congregants thanking the pastor for his prayers and their receipt of the miracle, rather than being able to thank him for an expository sermon and for the exegetical work he put into it, is not uncommon. This is promoted by hucksters. On and outside of television, viewers are asked to send in seed money in order to get the miracle they deserve. What is meant exactly by this use of miracle in those Christian circles that have made the meaning of a miracle so broad and casual?

The danger is that this sometimes demonstrates a widely accepted use of the concept that accommodates non-biblical ideas of spiritual matters. When one believes that miracles are widely occurring common place events, they are either engaging in self-delusion or never received or heard Biblical teaching on the topic. Sadly, people sometimes abandon belief along with the churches that may have advertised these events when disappointed.

In explanation to define a Biblical miracle, Vernon C. Grounds refers to 3 words used in the New Testament, δύναμις - power or miracle, τέρας - wonder or miracle, σημεῖον - sign or miracle. He makes these points:[14]

1. Sometimes used together (Acts 2:22ff.; 2 Thessalonians. 2:9; Hebrews 2:4).
2. Extraordinary, supernatural event related with the outworking of redemption, Hebraic or Christian. (John 2:9-11).3. They describe a supernatural work of God. (Exodus7:3 ff.; Deuteronomy 4:34, 35).
4. They authenticate revelatory agents and verify claims of God's communication, prophets and the Messiah. (1 Kings 18:39; John 3:2ff.; 9:32-33; Acts 10:38; Acts 13:6-12).
5. Designed to invoke faith and communicate His purpose. (Acts 2:22ff.; Hebrews 2:4).

---

14 Vernon C. Grounds, Baker's Dictionary of Theology, Everett Harrison, ed., Baker Book House, Grand Rapids, Michigan, 1978, page 356.

6. Can be by a Satanic agent. (Matthew 22:24; 2 Thessalonians 2:9).

In the New Testament, miracles are supernatural events, a means of special revelation and designed to bring about belief in the Messiah, which is God's redemptive purpose (John 17:3). Since the Bible has the only trustworthy record of miracles, why is it that there are so many being spoken of today? To assume miracles are plentifully continuing today, then it infers that Biblical Revelation is ongoing. Revelation[15] has ceased, the Canon is closed (Hebrews 1:1-2). The verb in verse 1, λαλήςᾶς (spoke) and verse 2 ἐλάλησεν (has spoken) are aorist tense. The root word λαλέω, means to *talk*, that is, *utter* words: —preach, say, speak (after), talk, tell, utter.[16] The aorist (completed action) is significant and overlooked, if a person believes that God speaks to them directly, the authority of the Scriptures is denied. He has spoken through the many means, appointed prophets and through the Lord Jesus Christ. Direction for believers is the written Word of God.

Fritz Rienecker comments regarding the words used in Hebrews 1:1-2:

---

15 Revelation is the unveiling of truth that would have been unknown otherwise. There are 2 means of revelation, general and special. They differ in mode, content, means and result. Special revelation: In general, God's Revelation has assumed a permanent form in the Scriptures. However, not all of the Bible is Special Revelation. Some things in the Bible would be known without it. Furthermore, all Special Revelation is not in the Bible. For instance, Paul's Mars Hill sermon (Acts 17) is summarized by Luke. Also, God has not revealed everything, but has given adequate knowledge (Deuteronomy 29:29). All of Jesus' words and actions are not recorded (John 21:25).
16 James Strong, Parsons Technology, Inc. Cedar Rapids, Iowa, electronic edition step files copyright © 1998, Strong's number 2980 λαλέω.

The aor. tense use of both God speaking by the prophets and also by His speaking by Christ indicates that God has finished speaking in both cases (Hughes).[17]

The Biblical understanding warns that deception may accompany these wondrous works, knowledge and signs that many may readily accept. The emphasis in the church is the gospel. The polemics that Paul and John warn about are claims of extra revelatory knowledge (1 Corinthians 12:3; Galatians 1:6-8; Colossians 2:8; 2 Thessalonians 2:10; 1 John 2:22 and 4:2-3). The cults always add to the Old and New Testament other written material claiming reliable knowledge (e.g. Watchtower Bible and Tract Society-Jehovah Witnesses, Latter Day Saints-Mormonism, Christian Science). Much of this material falls into the category of Gnosticism. These extra documents also include inferior translations of the Scripture and fictitious histories and claims they have prophets. We must be reminded that Gnosticism and its many forms grew out of and looking beyond God's sole revelation in the Scriptures (Revelation 22:18-19). To be sure, it is still around today and infects contemporary Christianity. A brief internet search will readily indicate this.

Alexander M. Renwick explains the impact of Gnosticism:

Many of its leading ideas had existed before the Christian era but its votaries felt that in the Christian religion were valuable elements which could be worked into their scheme of things. Their aim was to reduce Christianity to a philosophy and relate to various pagan teachings as well as to OT which they distorted. The term Gnostic comes from the Greek word *gnosis* which means "knowledge". The Gnostic claimed special esoteric of secret knowledge.[18]

---

17 Fritz Rienecker, trans., Cleon L. Rogers Jr., A Linguistic Key to the Greek New Testament Vol 2., Zondervan Publishing House, 1980, page 317.
18 Alexander M. Renwick, Baker's Dictionary of Theology, Everett Harrison, ed., Baker Book House, Grand Rapids, Michigan, 1978, page 237.

What is commonly observed and also not desirable is focusing on explaining what cannot be explained from human reasoning. After all, our discernment regarding the hidden matters of God is impossible (Deuteronomy 29:29). In some popular presentations from believers in modern day media, Christians may be heard recounting their experiences in terms of seeing the moves that God is making in their lives, or even seeing and claiming the guarantee of future events.

These ultimately are speculations from the reading of circumstances and redefining them to be clear indications of God's hidden will for them and might lead to wrong decisions. We can take comfort, as believers, that the Lord does concatenate all events for His purpose and love toward believers (Romans 8:38-39). It is treacherous to center on matters that we cannot discern in the circumstances in our lives. It is dangerous because one may fall into a chase to obtain an ideal will of God, its meaning and conclusions derived from good and bad circumstances that befall them.

Alvin Baker writes about God's secret will:

Now beyond a doubt, God knows what is best for each individual. In addition, He clearly has a plan for each individual, and it is His eternal plan. This plan, unlike the supposed ideal will, is certain to be fulfilled down to the smallest detail (Job 3:23; 14:5; 23:10; Psalm 139:16; Proverbs 16:9; Romans 8:28-30; Ephesians 1:11; 2:10). However, this will is basically "secret" (Deuteronomy 29:29) and believers are never exhorted to "find" or "discover" this secret will.[19]

Albert Barnes comments on Deuteronomy 29:29:

---

[19] Alvin L. Baker, 'Knowing the Will of God: Toward a Practical Theology Part I', page 28. (PDF download on 4/12/2018).

The secret things belong unto the LORD our God—This verse seems to be added as a solemn admonition on the part of Moses, in order to close the series of blessings and curses which he has delivered. The sense seems to be this: "The future, when and how these good and evil things will take effect, it lies with the Lord our God to determine; it pertains not to man's sphere and duty. God's revealed will is that which we must carry out." The 17th of our Articles of Religion concludes with much the same sentiment.[20]

We have all that is necessary in the Biblical Revelation "Christ the power of God and the wisdom of God." (1 Corinthians 1:22-24), it is sufficient and we should have the same desire as Jude "faith which was once for all handed down to the saints" (Jude 1:3).

Once a pastor spoke of another pastor, who claimed encountering a demonized woman on a city street. When questioned after the sermon, how did that pastor know that the person was demonized, the answer, "I don't know". And the other pastor's response to the demonized woman was hugging her and saying "Jesus loves you". Is saying, "Jesus loves you" even the gospel and would this be adequate to cast out the demon(s) and bring that women to faith? This perfunctory approach of just reciting Jesus' name is indicative of a naive, cursory and a jejune understanding of the New Testament and demonic possession. The serious nature of Satan and the demons is discussed by Robert Bennett, where he gives an exegetical analysis of the New Testament words and passages that apply to New Testament exorcism.

Robert Bennett says:

---

20 Albert Barnes, Barnes' Notes on the Old Testament- Deuteronomy, AGES Software Rio, WI USA Version 1.0 © 1999, comment on Deuteronomy 29:29. The Westminster Confession of Faith is referred to as to the 17th article.

There is one true power, namely, the triune God. If Satan possesses any power at all, it is only that which God has allowed him to exercise.[21]

Furthermore, the nature and activity of Satan and the demons is deception. To approach the topic with an off hand, superficial and casual manner indicates stark ignorance and denial of the New Testament literature. Always remember that the God of the Bible is sovereign over the spiritual realm (1 Kings 22:19-23; 2 Cor. 12:7).

Lewis Sperry Chafer best captures the attitude one should have when entering the topic of demonization:

Since Satan is the deceiver of the whole world, the truth about him, so far as his power may be exercised, will be veiled, distorted, and neglected; but, having explicit divine revelation by which to be guided, theologians, by seeming indifference, have no license to abet these forms of deception which involve spiritual tragedy of infinite and eternal import.[22]

Words like magic, special and sentimental dominate the conclusions around these observations heard in the churches. Sometimes stories of revivals that take place in other locations are presented, as if, the people of God should master in hearsay. That absence of expository preaching and theological knowledge in the church indicates the time we are in, 2 Timothy 4:2-4 "preach the word; be ready in season *and* out of season; reprove, rebuke, exhort, with great patience and instruction. For the time will come when they will not endure

---

21 Robert H. Bennett, I Am Not Afraid: Demon Possession And Spiritual Warfare, Concordia Publishing House, St Louis, Missouri, 2013, chap. 8, page 101.
22 Lewis Sperry Chafer, Systematic Theology, Vol I, Dallas Seminary Press, 1947, preface xxvii. Also: his treatment of Angelology in Vol. II, it is a excellent treatment of the subject.

sound doctrine; but *wanting* to have their ears tickled, they will accumulate for themselves teachers in accordance to their own desires, and will turn away their ears from the truth and will turn aside to myths."

The work of God has revealed the message for all to see. John 6:29 "Jesus answered and said to them, 'This is the work of God, that you believe in Him whom He has sent.'" God's work of regeneration cannot be controlled by us (John 3:8), "The wind blows where it wishes and you hear the sound of it, but do not know where it comes from and where it is going; so is everyone who is born of the Spirit." It has been noted that in some churches, a belief that if we can gather the right preachers and say the right prayers, have the right crowd size, get the lights, sound system, music and marketing right, we can guarantee evangelical success.

But, when the gospel is proclaimed the power of God is demonstrated. (1 Corinthians 2:4-5; 1 Thessalonians 1:5). The nature of God's life for the believer is prolific and iterative and is based on the Word of God (Matthew 18:3; 2 Peter 1:4).

Remember faith is external to the Christian. It is a gift from God. Paul is teaching us of our need for the righteousness of God, it is not our own (Ephesians 2:8-9). Martin Luther and the term he uses "alien righteousness" summarizes this concept.[23] Additionally, any sympathy on the Christian's part to trust in our feelings and look inward for religious guidance is warned against in the Bible (Jeremiah 17:9, Proverbs 3:5-6, 14:12-13, 28:26).

---

23 John Dillenberger, ed., Two kinds of Righteousness, Martin Luther Selections From His Writings, Anchor Books, Doubleday & Company, Inc, Garden City, New York, 1961, page 86.

People will always readily line up to receive miracles, healing and come to banquets showcasing special motivation speakers and gladly pay for a ticket. But how many will acknowledge the Savior? The account of the healing of the 10 lepers in Luke 17:11-19 records, one only returning to worship God, readily demonstrates the point. Nine were interested in the healing, but the one returned and gave thanks and was interested in the Christ of the healing. Jesus' response indicated that this one was saved, not simply in body but in soul. It is not clear if the others came to faith. This is consistent with God's mercy, He shows mercy to all, Luke 6:35 "But love your enemies, and do good, and lend, expecting nothing in return; and your reward will be great, and you will be sons of the Most High; for He Himself is kind to ungrateful and evil *men*".

Chapter 2
Need of The Righteousness of God

CONDEMNATION OF JEWS
PRINCIPLES OF JUDGMENT
2:6   PSALM 62:12

HISTORIC FAILURE OF THE JEWS
2:24   ISAIAH 52:5; [EZEKIEL 36:20FF.]

In chapter 2, there are 2 citations from Psalms and Isaiah. Paul has condemned the heathen and continues on to the condemnation of the Jews. It would be natural to use the Old Testament when addressing the Jews. The Psalms and Isaiah are most cited in the New Testament and very familiar with Jews from the synagogue. But both parties are condemned by Paul because he has included the Gentile world in condemnation in Romans 1:18.

Paul moves on to the Righteousness of God in Salvation, man's need of this Righteousness of God, by condemning both the heathen and the Jews since all men are under condemnation (Romans 2:9). He uses the Old Testament to demonstrate his teaching.

PRINCIPLES OF JUDGMENT
2:6   PSALM 62:12

A quote from Psalm 62:12. All men are condemned in this summary in Romans 2:6 "who WILL RENDER TO EACH PERSON ACCORDING TO HIS DEEDS". ότι συ αποδώσεις εκάστω κατά τα έργα αυτού, vid., LXX). It is the moral quality of our decisions that will be the basis of judgment of the world (Romans 2:16). This is the *Law* coming from Psalms and its *first use*, or moral rule aspect, but however adds an eschatological promise. For categorical purposes, it is observed this is a combination use of the *Law in its first sense,* but however, adds a *prophetic* promise of eschatological fulfillment of judgment.

Archibald M'Caig details the usage from the article in the 'Law in the Epistles' this way:

(1) *Law as a standard.*-In Romans Paul has much to say about law, and in the main it is the moral law that he has in view. In this great epistle, written to people at the center of the famous legal system of Rome, many of them Jews versed in the law of Moses and others Gentiles familiar with the idea of law, its nature, its scope and its sway, he first speaks of the Law as a standard, want of conformity to which brings condemnation. He shows that the Gentiles who had not the standard of the revealed Law nevertheless had a law, the law of Nature, a law written upon their heart and conscience.[24]

Make no mistake works do not save men. W. L. Walker makes this important distinction:

"Works" is used by Paul and James, in a special sense, as denoting (with Paul) those legal performances by means of which men sought to be accepted of God, in contradistinction to that faith in Christ through which the sinner is justified apart from all legal works, (Rom 3:27; 4:2, 6, etc.; Gal 2:16; 3:2, 5, 10).[25]

This devotional and wisdom Psalm is used by Paul to continue his argument that the righteousness of God is necessary for salvation. No man possesses God's righteousness, so it must be

---

24 Archibald M'Caig, gen. ed., James Orr, International Standard Bible Encyclopedia, Volume III, Wm. B. Eerdmans Publishing Grand Rapids, Michigan, reprinted 1978, page 1848.
25 W. L. Walker, gen. ed., James Orr,, International Standard Bible Encyclopedia, Volume V, Wm. B. Eerdmans Publishing Grand Rapids, Michigan, reprinted 1978, page 3105.

given to him. A man doesn't receive God's righteousness unless he is certain that he needs to.

This combination of categories, *Law* in its *first use, condemnation,* a demonstration of the shortfall of all men. For the believer, the *second use of the Law* that prompts the need for remedy, and also the *third use,* a regulatory guide. Finally, Romans 2:6, is also seen as *prophetic* in judgment.

This shortfall, that applies to all, can become a stumbling point and creates a dilemma for some Christians and church goers, because it is ever present, even after conversion. When a distortion of balance develops between knowing that you are a sinner, having faith, grasping justification, but fear of falling into antinomianism and in opposition to that fear, motivation ensues to rack up points of good behavior as if the points would gain God's approbation granting adequate standing before God, thus creating a self originated system of justification. Many times church goers have been heard saying, "When I die I hope I'm good enough to go to heaven." This point of understanding the gospel must be reached, that you are not good enough and never will be, according to the perfect standard of the Law (Galatians 2:21).

There is also another danger in this thinking caused by this conflict of the two natures. Ecclesiastical eulogies sometimes speak on how good the man or woman was, who just died. That reinforces the idea that one can earn their way to acceptance by God. These are not Christ centered eulogies and will lead to a soft universalism, everyone is saved in the end, because the standard of righteousness somehow becomes an individualized matter. Churches then begin to accept this heterodoxy. The question always arises, to what extent does heterodoxy carry a church or individual into heresy and outside of the orthodox understanding of justification by faith alone?

Representing the Lutheran Reformation view of the Law of God, The Formula of Concord states:

The Law was given to men for three reasons: first, that thereby outward discipline might be maintained against wild, disobedient men [and that wild and intractable men might be restrained, as though by certain bars]; secondly, that men thereby may be led to the knowledge of their sins; thirdly, that after they are regenerate and [much of] the flesh notwithstanding cleaves to them, they might on this account have a fixed rule according to which they are to regulate and direct their whole life.[26] (cf. first:1 Timothy 1:8ff.; Romans 3:20; second:. Galatians 3:24ff.; third: Ephesians 2:8-10)

The observation of these distinctions of the Law's use in Romans, always must be seen as redemptive, in that, stating the horrible and depraved condition of the Jews and Gentiles, which is expressed in the *Law's first use* is inevitably designed to lead the hearer to salvation (*second use*-Romans 3:20) through faith in Christ, the remedy that God has given. Civil government law codes recognize the need for law and order and derive their authority from the *first use of the Law*.

His presentation is also structured to demonstrate what the *first use of the Law* is intended to do, that the *Law in its first use* cannot give salvation but only condemns (Galatians 2:21).

In his letter to Timothy, Paul reminds us of his personal history and the knowledge of *condemnation the Law* gave him, Timothy 1;13, "even though I was formerly a blasphemer and a persecutor and a violent aggressor. Yet I was shown mercy because I acted ignorantly in unbelief." Some of us are as bad as him, maybe some worse than him, but all those who live by

---

[26] The Formula of Concord, Concordia Publishing House 2005, (Epitome VI. 1). page 504.

faith understand we are as bad off as Paul was without faith in the gospel, that gives us what we don't have on our own. The response to the *first use* (condemnation) of the Law is the *second* (remediation) and *third* (regulation) applied to some people but not all (Matthew 7:13-14).

HISTORIC FAILURE OF THE JEWS
2:24   ISAIAH 52:5; [EZEKIEL 36:20FF.]

Not only are the Gentiles condemned due to their works, but the Jews demonstrate the same problem, to a worse magnitude. Romans 2:24 is citation from Isaiah 52:5 and some similarity to Ezekiel 36:20ff. The Jews are condemned in this summary, referencing their historically notoriously bad behavior. "For 'THE NAME OF GOD IS BLASPHEMED AMONG THE GENTILES BECAUSE OF YOU,' just as it is written." (ὑμᾶς διαπαντός τo ὀνομάμου βλασφημεῖται ἐν τοῖς ἔθνεσιν, vid., LXX).

Heinrich Meyer comments on Romans 2:24:

The phrase 'βλασφημεῖται ἐν τοῖς ἔθνεσιν' *among the Gentiles,* inasmuch, namely, as these infer from the immoral conduct of the Jews that they have an unholy God and Lawgiver, and are thereby moved to blaspheme His holy name.[27]

Heinrich Meyer also points out that Paul uses "as it is written" is following after the citation, the only place (see Appendix III) Paul does this:

But he applies the quotation in such a way that he makes it his own by the γάρ not found in the original or the LXX.; only indicating by καθὼς γέγραπται at the close, that he has thus appropriated a passage

---

27 H. A. W. Meyer's, Critical and Exegetical Commentary on the New Testament, Romans, Vol. V., Alpha Greek Library, Winona Lake Wisconsin, reprinted 1980, page 101.

of Scripture. Hence καθὼς γέγ. is placed at the end, as is never done in the case of express quotations of Scripture. The historical sense (It refers to God's name being dishourned through the enslaving of the Jews by their tyrants) of the passage is not here concerned, since Paul has not quoted it as a fulfilled prophecy, though otherwise with propriety in the sense of Romans 3:19.[28]

Paul is using the Old Testament, in a *historical* sense and to corroborate his testimony. It is a documented record of the bad conduct of the Jews.

Here in Isaiah 52:5 and Ezekiel 36:20ff. is the *historical* documentation of the failure of the Jews. Paul answers anticipated objections for the condemnation he pronounced upon them. God's word of salvation given through the Jews does not automatically exempt the Jews or anyone else from judgment in the promises of God, even if they are not believed. Faith is from the Lord, it is not a human product. Even if everyone on the earth believed that God doesn't exist, nothing changed about Him and His character and promises (Isaiah 40:18, 25). Here, the Jews in possession of the oracles of God and that great advantage does not exempt from God's judgment, if the gift of faith is rejected. So what, nothing has changed. The promises of salvation and judgment are in force and still available.

These Old Testament citations (Isaiah 52:5; Ezekiel 36:20ff.) serve as a confirmation of the character of God and refutation of the opposition argument, Romans 2:17, "But if you bear the name 'Jew' and rely upon the Law and boast in God", from the very oracles that the Jews possess. Failure to take advantage of a gift doesn't automatically maintain possession of the gift.

Franz Delitzsch, epitomizes the argument:

---

[28] Ibid., page 100-101.

And it is just the nature of penitence so to confess one's self to be in the wrong in order that God may be in the right and gain His cause. If, however, the sinner's self-accusation justifies the divine righteousness or justice, just as, on the other hand, all self-justification on the part of the sinner (which, however, sooner or later will be undeceived) accuses God of unrighteousness or injustice (Job 40:8): then all human sin must in the end tend towards the glorifying of God.[29]

---

[29] F. Delitzsch, trans. Francis Bolton, Commentary on the Old Testament Vol. V, second section: Psalms, Wm. B. Eerdmans Publishing Grand Rapids, Michigan, reprinted 1979, second Volume page 136.

Chapter 3
Condemnation of all men

Answers to the Jews
3:4   Psalm 51:4

Condemnation of all men
3:10-12   Psalm 14:1; 53:1-4
3:13   Psalm 5:9; 140:3
3:14   Psalm 10:7
3:15-17   Isaiah 59:7
3:18   Psalm 36:1

In chapter 3, the Old Testament citations are also from Psalms and Isaiah. Paul is behaving like a prosecutor in a court of Law by bringing expert testimony to bear. Here, the Word of God from the Old Testament is on the witness stand giving testimony on behalf of the accused, God. Roles are reversed, ironically the condemned are accusing the condemner.

Answers to the Jews
3:4   Psalm 51:4

Romans 3:4 citation is from the LXX, Psalm 51:4. The phrase *May it never be!*, μὴ γένοιτο is used by Paul 15 times (10 times in Romans; once in 1 Corinthians; 3 times in Galatians). The only writer besides Paul is Luke, that uses *May it never be!* (Luke 20:16). Paul writes, Rather, let God be found true, though every man be found a liar, as it is written, "THAT YOU MAY BE JUSTIFIED IN YOUR WORDS, AND PREVAIL WHEN YOU ARE JUDGED." The first part of the verse is penitential in nature as is the Psalm "Against You, You only, I have sinned And done what is evil in Your sight." The possibility that the unbelief could have the power to impugn the character of God is rejected in the strongest possible manner. The preface to his argument begins with the righteous character of God opposed to man's depravity. This will be true, it is continuing *prophetic* word.

Henry Alford puts it this way:

'The Apostle uses this expression of pious horror, when he has supposed or mentioned any thing by which the honour, truth, or justice of God would be compromised, as hereby His covenant-word being broken.' [30]

Unlike mankind, the Scripture asserts that God is ethically pure and holy. He is separate from sin and evil and has no communion with sin (Job 34:10; Isaiah 6:3). He has the attribute of veracity. The phrase γινώσκω δέ ὅ θεῖος ἀληθής (let God be found true) and the use of the word true implies the "real state of affairs."[31] and means "'trustworthy or reliable".[32]

The truth of God is the foundation of all knowledge, things really are the way they really are, therefore, man can know reality or truth about something. Truth is unequivocal, and unambiguous. Unlike Philosophical skepticism, the Scripture speaks with certainty. As John 14:6 states, Jesus said to him, "I am the way, and the truth, and the life; no one comes to the Father, but through Me." The conclusion that Jewish unbelief nullifies God's faithfulness is impossible and is to be rejected in the strongest possible terms. Paul places the foundation of his forensic argument with the character of God. There is no

---

30 Henry Alford, Alford's Greek New Testament, Vol., II Baker Book House, Grand Rapids, Michigan, reprint 1980, page 338.
31 Rudolf Bultmann, ed. Gerhard Kittel, trans. Geoffrey Bromiley, (TDNT) Theological Dictionary of the New Testament Vol. I, Wm. B. Eerdmans Publishing Grand Rapids, Michigan, reprinted 1979 10th printing 1979, page 243.
32 Ibid., page 248.

exemption from judgment by making wrong conclusions, for Jews and Gentiles.

As Heinrich Meyer capsulizes what the Apostle is saying, it must be seen in context as *prophetic*, when the continued thought by Paul, includes:

His truthfulness is to be the actual result produced (namely, in the carrying out of His Messianic plan of salvation), *and every man a liar.* To this it *shall* come; the development of the holy divine economy to this final state of the relation between God and men, is what Paul knows and *wishes*.... '*the historical result* which shall *come to pass*, the *actual Theodicée* that shall *take place'*[33]

Ernest Burton details the mood and tense of μὴ γένοιτο:

The phrase **mh genoito** is an Optative of Wishing which strongly deprecates something suggested by a previous question or assertion. Fourteen of the fifteen New Testament instances are in Paul's writings, and in twelve of these it expresses the apostle's abhorrence of an inference which he fears may be (falsely) drawn from his argument.[34]

CONDEMNATION OF ALL MEN
3:10-12	PSALM 14:1; 53:1-4
3:13	PSALM 5:9; 140:3
3:14	PSALM 10:7
3:15-17	ISAIAH 59:7
3:18	PSALM 36:1

In Romans 3:10-18,

---

33 H. A. W. Meyer's, Critical and Exegetical Commentary on the New Testament, Romans, Vol. V., Alpha Greek Library, Winona Lake Wisconsin, reprinted 1980, page 113.
34 Ernest De Witt Burton, Syntax Of The Moods And Tenses In New Testament Greek, The University of Chicago Press Chicago, Illinois, 1900, page 79.

⁹ What then? Are we better than they? Not at all; for we have already charged that both Jews and Greeks are all under sin; ¹⁰ as it is written,
> "There is none righteous, not even one;
¹¹ THERE IS NONE WHO UNDERSTANDS,
THERE IS NONE WHO SEEKS FOR GOD;
¹² ALL HAVE TURNED ASIDE, TOGETHER THEY HAVE BECOME USELESS;
There is none who does good,
THERE IS NOT EVEN ONE."
¹³ "THEIR THROAT IS AN OPEN GRAVE,
With their tongues they keep deceiving,"
"THE POISON OF ASPS IS UNDER THEIR LIPS";
¹⁴ "WHOSE MOUTH IS FULL OF CURSING AND BITTERNESS";
¹⁵ "THEIR FEET ARE SWIFT TO SHED BLOOD,
¹⁶ DESTRUCTION AND MISERY ARE IN THEIR PATHS,
¹⁷ AND THE PATH OF PEACE THEY HAVE NOT KNOWN."
¹⁸ "THERE IS NO FEAR OF GOD BEFORE THEIR EYES."

Paul asserts and reiterates the universal condemnation of all men. The first witnesses are from the most frequently used Old Testament references in the New Testament, Psalms and Isaiah (taken from LXX). His case presents this way, assertion and inculpating evidence. These witnesses testify that the indictees demonstrate their culpability and offer no ability to be justified by their works. Sin is *pervasive* 3:10-12, (Psalm 14:1; 53:1-4), *demonstrated through speech* 3:13-14 (Psalm 5:9; 140:3; 10:7) and further *through deeds* 3:15-17 (Isaiah 59:7), the cause is due to *mindset* 3:18 (Psalm 36:1). Paul is in a trial mode, a witness on the stand giving testimony The witness is the the Old Testament. Romans 3:19-20, testifies to their guilt before the Law of God, the *Law's first use*. The word ὑπόδικος (accountable, guilty, under sentence v. 19), is an old forensic word here only in N. T. Everyone is liable to God in God's court.'[35] Paul referring to the Gentile and Jews uses the word προῃτιασάμεθα, (charged, proved, v. 9) "a word not yet found anywhere else".[36]

Marvin Vincent explains it this way:

We have before proved (προῃτιασάμεθα) 'The reference is not to logical proof, but to forensic accusation. The simple verb means *to charge* as being *the cause* (αἰτία) of some evil: hence *to accuse, impeach*.'[37]

This stage of the prosecution is complete, in the next stage, he goes on to further elaborate justification by faith. Next will be, Abraham and David who are historic persons of record as witnesses for Paul's testimony.

---

35 A. T. Robertson, Word Pictures in the New Testament, Vol. IV, The Epistles of Paul, Baker Book House, Grand Rapids, Michigan, 1931, page 346.
36 Ibid,, page 344.
37 Marvin R. Vincent, Vincent's Word Studies, Vol. 3, The Epistles of Paul: Romans, Corinthians, Ephesians, Philippians, Colossians, Philemon, Parsons Technology, Inc. Hiawatha, Iowa, electronic edition step files copyright © 1998.

Chapter 4
Illustration of Justification from Old Testament

JUSTIFICATION IS ONLY BY FAITH BY EXAMPLE OF ABRAHAM
4:3 GENESIS 15:6

JUSTIFICATION IS ONLY BY FAITH BY EXAMPLE OF KING DAVID
4:7-8 PSALM 32:1-2

JUSTIFICATION IS NOT DEPENDENT ON THE RITE OF CIRCUMCISION
4:9 GENESIS 15:6

PROPHECY CONCERNING ABRAHAM'S DESCENDANTS
4:17 GENESIS 17:5

HIS FAITH CORRESPONDS TO THE PROMISE OF GOD
4:18 GENESIS 15:5
HIS FAITH IS REWARDED BY GRACE
4:22 GENESIS 15:6

In Romans chapter 4, Paul starts by going back and citing Genesis 15:6. Invoking the historical record and the authority of the Old Testament Paul starts with a rhetorical question, which he uses in this epistle (4:1; 6:1; 7:7; 8:31; 9:14, 30), probably methodology from his rabbinical days and a method that is still used in teaching methodology to this day. Justification is only by faith 4:1-5.

JUSTIFICATION IS ONLY BY FAITH BY EXAMPLE OF ABRAHAM
4:3 GENESIS 15:6

The example of Abraham reiterates what has previously been said (Romans 1:17), salvation comes by means of faith and not by works. In 4:2, the clause, εἰ γὰρ Ἀβραὰμ ἐξ ἔργων ἐδικαιώθη (for if Abraham out of works was saved), εἰ (if) coupled with the indicative ἐδικαιώθη (was justified) from δικαιόω (justified), a condition of the first class (condition of fact) is used.[38] To clarify, the condition of fact accepts the fact whether proved true or not for the use of the argument. However, Paul's teaching indicates that works cannot justify, Abraham's works vanish before God's standards.

Archibald Robertson remarking on Romans 4:2:

Condition of first class, assumed as true for the sake of argument, though untrue in fact. The rabbis had a doctrine of the merits of Abraham who had a superfluity of credits to pass on to the Jews (Luke 3:8).[39]

and, Abraham believed God (v. 3),
'It was set down on the credit side of the ledger "for" (*eis* as often) righteousness. What was set down? His believing God (*episteusen toôi theoôi*).'[40]

Abraham being justified out of his own efforts is erroneous to believe. In verses 4-6, Paul makes his point by writing, God credits righteousness apart from works.

Cleon Rogers on the use of justified writes:

The use of ἐλογίσθη (from λογίζομαι (justified v. 3)), is the language of an accountant and entry into a ledger, 'faith is not the equivalent of righteousness, but God is giving a status of righteousness to Abraham.'[41]

---

38 J. Harold Greenlee, A Concise Exegetical Grammar of New Testament Greek, Wm. B. Eerdmans Publishing Grand Rapids, Michigan, reprinted 1979, page 71.
39 A. T. Robertson, Word Pictures in the New Testament, Vol. IV, The Epistles of Paul, Baker Book House, Grand Rapids, Michigan, 1931, page 350.
40 Ibid.

He introduces the next Old Testament citation (Romans 4:3) from the LXX, with "For what does the Scripture say?", the only other time he use this sentence in his writings is Galatians 4:30. In the New Testament, γὰρ ἡ γραφὴ λέγει, "for the Scripture says", is used (John 19:17; Romans 9:17, 10:11,11:12; 1 Timothy 5:18). It contains the all important, ἡ γραφὴ, the Scripture, holy writ.

The question is, what exactly did Abraham believe? Starting in Genesis 12, Abraham received divine revelation. Charles Feinberg writes of the word used in Genesis 12:1 אָמַר, aòmar, "said":

The word 'amar' is used repeatedly by God to introduce revelation. One would suppose that this usage emphasizes that God's revelation is a spoken, transmissible, propositional, definite matter. The "word" does not make it a revelation. God gives the revelation to persons as one person imparts knowledge to another-by spoken word.[42]

In Genesis 15:1, Abraham received direct special revelation in a night vision. The phrase "word of the Lord" in the MT, יְהוָה, (yehoòvaòh,yeh-ho-vaw') דָּבָר, (daòbaòr,daw-bawr') 'word' coupled with the tetragrammaton appears only 9 times in the Pentateuch. It is a technical term for the prophetic word of revelation.[43]

---

41 Cleon Rogers Jr., Cleon Rogers III, A Linguistic Key and Exegetical Key to the Greek New Testament, Zondervan Publishing House, 1998, page 323.
42 Charles L. Feinberg, William White, ed., R. Laird Harris, (TWOT) Theological Wordbook of the Old Testament, Vol 2, Moody press, Chicago, 1980, page 55.
43 W. H Schmidt, eds., G. Johannes Botterweck, Helmer Ringgren, trans., John T. Willis, (TDOT) Theological Dictionary of the Old Testament, Vol III, Wm. B. Eerdmans Publishing Company, Grand Rapids, MI 1974, page 111.

Abraham was given the promise of an offspring at age 75 (Genesis 12:4). At age 86 (Genesis 16:16), Hagar gives birth to Ishmael, from the result of prompting of his wife Sarai since she was barren (Genesis 11:30). It is probably not a presumption to believe that God's promise of children and descendants prompted this activity. Ishmael is not the son of promise, Isaac is. Abraham is 100 years of age (Genesis 21:5) when Isaac is born.

After the flood, gradually, longevity of humankind began to decline, so Abraham's virility and longevity is nothing like those prior to the flood and after the Fall of Mankind (cf. Genesis 5 with Genesis 6:3 and Deuteronomy 34:7). The promised fulfilled through Abraham become the indicator that God performs His promises (Romans 4:19-21). Abraham's faith is in God and not in himself, as to his inability, impotency and atrophy as concerns procreation. Sarah is not capable of conception. Abraham's faith and experience is our model of faith, God brings life from the dead. Just as we are impotent and unable to extricate ourselves from the curse and deadness made by sin, God delivers us through His life giving power. Abraham is a regenerate man. Paul says he believes the promises of God, he has faith, that is sufficient.

Abraham's saga must be examined more fully. Particularly the sacrifice of Isaac. Genesis chapter 22 and Hebrews chapter 11 should be examined to answer question about this sacrifice.

Abraham is commanded to sacrifice Isaac in Genesis 22. Genesis 22:5 states he gave instructions to his young men, "Stay here with the donkey, and I and the lad will go over there; and we will worship and return to you." He fully intended to sacrifice Isaac as a burnt offering believing God would raise him from the dead. He continued as commanded until God stopped him. Hebrews 11:19, "He considered that God is able to raise *people* even from the dead, from which he also received him back as a type." (ἐν παραβολῇ "in a type", parable).

Friedrich Hauck clarifies the meaning of παραβολῇ used here:

> In Hb. παραβολῇ means "counterpart" or "type", Hb. 9:9: The former tabernacle is a figurative intimation of the heavenly tabernacle. According to Hb. 11:19 the returning of Isaac to Abraham was a likeness pointing beyond itself. It represented future awakening from the dead.[44]

The Biblical record is clear, Abraham actually intended to sacrifice Isaac. He also expected to return with Issac. His experience is also revelation of Christ's resurrection after death.

Note the 3 equivalent Hebrew to Greek words concerned with when speaking of Abraham and what attributed to his believing.

Genesis 15:6	Romans 4:3, 8, 22 (v. 22 faith omitted)
אָמַן aòman	πίστεως pisteuoô faith, belief, trust
צְדָקָה tsedaòqaòh'	δικαιοσύνην dikaiosuneô justification, justify, right(ness)
חָשַׁב chaòshab	λογίζομαι logizomai count, reckon, credit, impute

The words in the Old Testament and the New Testament equivalents, form the sine qua non, of the Christian faith.

---

44 Friedrich Hauck, ed. Gerhard Kittel, trans. Geoffrey Bromiley, (TDNT) Theological Dictionary of the New Testament Vol. V, Wm. B. Eerdmans Publishing Grand Rapids, Michigan, reprinted 1979 10th printing 1979, page 752.

James I. Packer makes 3 summary statements about 'faith' πίστεως [45].
1. Faith in God involves right belief about God.
2. Faith rests on Divine testimony.
3. Faith is a supernatural Divine gift.

and he states this regarding justification, δικαιοσύνην:

The basic fact of biblical religion is that God pardons and accepts believing sinners ... the doctrine of justification determines the whole character of Christianity as a religion of grace and faith.[46]

Abraham, Paul makes clear, does not have any reason to boast. Man does not possess the righteousness that God demands. He cannot get it on his own nor has the power to self extricate from this condition and lacks moral ability (Ephesians 2:1,8-9). God is the giver of righteousness, man cannot get it by earning or working for it and Abraham did not. It sources from God (1 Peter 1:23). God grants righteousness to any man by His own accounting, using faith as the gift and means to obtain the righteousness of God. Abraham as a prime example of believing God. This is justification (λογίζομαι). Romans 4:3 contains the promise of justification by faith is therefore *prophetic* and ongoing throughout the church age.

The illustration would follow like this. You are charged and found guilty of condemnable, multiplicity of crimes, the nature and magnitude of these warrant the death penalty. You arrive in court. Jesus seated as judge reads the entire list of crimes and subsequent penalties due. When He as judge, John 5:22 "For not even the Father judges anyone, but He has given all judgment to the Son", is ready to pronounce guilt and the

---

[45] James I. Packer, ed. E. F. Harrison, Baker's Dictionary of Theology, Baker Book House, Grand Rapids, Michigan, 1978, pp. 209-210.
[46] Ibid., page 303.

penalty due, He takes off His robes and stands in place of the condemned sinner.

Jesus then takes the penalty for sinners as the judge and substitute (Isaiah 53:4-5). He is condemning himself. He will receive the penalty that is due in your place, "the defendant is covered I know him", Jesus says. The Judge accepts the substitution because the law must be satisfied and the penalties paid (cf. John 5:22; Romans 5:6; Colossians 2:13-14). A defendant that comes into the court with comprehensive charges like yours, would not want to be in a place where Jesus does not stand up for him.

Regarding λογίζομαι, Louis Berkhof's definition goes this way:

Justification is a judicial act of God, in which He declares, on the basis of the righteousness of Jesus Christ, that all the claims of the law are satisfied in respect of the sinner.[47]

The method that God uses is imputation, as Caspar Hodge writes:

The word "imputation," according to the Scriptural usage, denotes an attributing of something to a person, or a charging of one with anything, or a setting of something to one's account. This takes place sometimes in a judicial manner, so that the thing imputed becomes a ground of reward or punishment.[48]

---

47 Louis Berkhof, Systematic Theology, Wm. B. Eerdmans, Publishing Grand Rapids, Michigan, reprinted 1977, page 513.
48 Caspar Wistar Hodge, gen. ed., James Orr, International Standard Bible Encyclopedia, Volume III, Wm. B. Eerdmans Publishing Grand Rapids, Michigan, reprinted 1978, page 1462.

The means to apprehend this is faith, a supernatural and divine gift.[49] Examples from the Scripture include Ephesians 2:8-9, Acts 16:14 and Luke 23:43. Paul is presenting that we do not possess the righteousness of God and must obtain it by means of faith (Romans 1:17). Luther captures this Apostolic teaching as "alien righteousness"[50], it is outside ourselves and it must be given by God to us. It is also important to observe that Paul uses Genesis 15:6 three times in his assertion., "Then he believed in the LORD; and He reckoned it to him as righteousness".

In modern political religious speech it is popular to say, "There are three religions that claim Abraham as their father, the Jews, Islam and Christianity". The Jews have rejected the Messiah, Islam denies the deity of Christ. Only Christianity can claim Abraham as the Father of the faith.

JUSTIFICATION IS ONLY BY FAITH BY EXAMPLE OF KING DAVID
4:7-8 PSALM 32:1-2

In Romans 4:6-8, iteration to the previous argument, with a new witness. As with Abraham before the Law was given, justification by faith is also taught in the Old Testament by King David, after the Law was given. It is in opposition to teaching works as a means to obtain righteous standing before God. From the LXX, Paul uses the Davidic Psalm 32:1-2. "BLESSED ARE THOSE WHOSE LAWLESS DEEDS HAVE BEEN FORGIVEN, AND WHOSE SINS HAVE BEEN COVERED. BLESSED IS THE MAN WHOSE SIN THE LORD WILL NOT TAKE INTO ACCOUNT." King David is a prime example of a lawless sinner being justified

---

49 James I. Packer, ed. E. F. Harrison, Baker's Dictionary of Theology, Baker Book House, Grand Rapids, Michigan, 1978, page 210.
50 John Dillenberger, ed., Two Kinds of Righteousness, Martin Luther Selections From His Writings, Anchor Books, Doubleday & Company, Inc, Garden City, New York, 1961, page 86.

and is seen in the *third use of the Law,* and the sinner receiving the effects of justification and its benefit as a guide.

Karl Keil and Franz Delitzsch comment on this Psalm, connecting also the Church Father Augustine and affinity with King David's experience:

... Ps 32 is a didactic Psalm, concerning the way of penitence which leads to the forgiveness of sins; it is the second of the seven *Psalmi paenitentiales* of the church, and Augustine's favourite Psalm. We might take Augustine's words as its motto: *intelligentia prima est ut te noris peccatorem.* The poet bases it upon his own personal experience, and then applies the general teaching which he deduces from it, to each individual in the church of God. For a whole year after his adultery David was like one under sentence of condemnation. In the midst of this fearful anguish of soul he composed Ps 51, whereas Ps 32 was composed after his deliverance from this state of mind.[51]

JUSTIFICATION IS NOT DEPENDENT ON THE RITE OF CIRCUMCISION
4:9   GENESIS 15:6

As much as circumcision is prescribed as a sign and external rite of the covenant with Abraham (Genesis 17:11), it also is to indicate an internal change (Deuteronomy 10:16 and 30:6). To simply leave the impact of circumcision as external, nullifies the entire Pauline teaching (Colossians 2:11), that justification is not dependent on it. Paul included circumcision in his credentials, (Philippians 3:5) but never asserted that it justifies. The impact of a life of faith is seen as the *third use of the Law.*

---

51 C. F. Keil & F. Delitzsch, trans. James Martin, Commentary on the Old Testament Vol. 5 Psalms, Wm. B. Eerdmans Publishing Grand Rapids, Michigan, reprinted 1980, page 393, first section. (intelligentia prima etc., 'the beginning of knowledge is to know oneself to be a sinner').

This justification is not dependent on the rite of circumcision (4:9) For we say, "FAITH WAS CREDITED TO ABRAHAM AS RIGHTEOUSNESS."

PROPHECY CONCERNING ABRAHAM'S DESCENDANTS
4:17   GENESIS 17:5

Building on his use of Genesis 15:6, he elaborates and states that, justification is apart from the Law (4:13-17). It is important to reiterate that in the sequence of revelation, Abraham existed before the Mosaic code and King David after the Mosaic code.

W. Sanday, A. C. Headlam commenting on this section of chapter 4:13-17:

13-17. In this section St. Paul brings up the key-words of his own system Faith, Promise, Grace, and marshals them in array over against the the leading points in the current theology of the Jews Law, Works or performance of Law. Because the working of this latter system had been so disastrous, ending only in condemnation, it was a relief to find that it was not what God had really intended, but that the true principles of things held out a prospect so much brighter and more hopeful, and one which furnished such an abundant justification for all that seemed new in Christianity.[52]

Another condition of the first class is used (v. 14, assumed true for argument but untrue in fact). The promise to Abraham is from faith in the promise of God, which predates the concept of the Law that the Jews are operating with. Paul's logic points out that if being an heir is dependent on law, which did not exist at

---

52 W. Sanday, A. C. Headlam, The International Critical Commentary, Critical and Exegetical Commentary on the Epistle to the Romans Edinburgh: T & T Clark, 1902, page 110.

the time of the given promise, then the Jews cannot be heirs based on Law, because of its non existence.

Frederic Godet makes this point regarding verse 15:

Simply because the law, when not fulfilled, brings on man God's disapprobation, *wrath,* which renders it impossible on His part to fulfill the promise.[53]

If this were to be true, those of the Law are heirs, it follows that faith is made void also. That is why it is by faith only.

James Denney explains:

For (Romans 4:14) if those who are of law, i.e., Jews only, as partisans of Law, are heirs, then faith (the correlative of promise) has been made vain, and the promise of no effect. And this incompatibility of law and promise in idea is supported by the actual effect of the Law in human experience. For the law works wrath—the very opposite of promise. But where there is not Law, there is not even transgression, still less the wrath which transgression provokes. Here, then, the other series of conceptions finds its sphere: the world is ruled by grace, promise and faith. This is the world in which Abraham lived, and in which all believers live; and as its typical citizen, he is father of them all.[54]

In verse 17, Paul restates that Abraham is the father of those that have faith in the promise of God. The use of καθὼς γέγραπται appears again, referencing Genesis 17:5, proving what he says from the Old Testament, this is *prophetic* and also proleptic as God is looking from Abraham into the ages to see

---

53 Frederic Godet, St Paul's Epistle to the Roman Theological Library. trans. A Cusin, new series., Vol. I, Edinburgh: T & T Clark, 38 George Street. 1881, page 298.
54 James Denney, ed. W. Robertson Nicoll, The Expositor's Greek Testament, Vol. II, Wm. B. Eerdmans Publishing Grand Rapids, Michigan, reprinted 1979, page 618.

the fruit of His work. The proof is that this promise brings life from death.

As Archibald Robertson describes it this way:

Summons the non-existing as existing." Abraham's body was old and decrepit. God rejuvenated him and Sarah (Heb 11:19).'[55]

HIS FAITH CORRESPONDS TO THE PROMISE OF GOD
4:18   GENESIS 15:5

HIS FAITH IS REWARDED BY GRACE
4:22   GENESIS 15:6

Paul further asserts that the character of Abraham's faith (4:18-22), corresponds to the promise of God, "SO SHALL YOUR DESCENDANTS BE.", (4:18), extends to the improbable (4:19), creates confidence (4:20), and strengthens faith (4:21), is imputed because of grace (4:22). Faith in a resurrecting God and Lord (4:23-24), comes from Abraham's account, the spiritual father of our faith and brings us to faith in a substitutionary Savior (4:25). In verse 22, he reiterates from Genesis 15:6, what he used in verse 3.

The uses here by Paul of the Old Testament citations (4:18,22) must seen seen as *prophecy* and ongoing *prophetic fulfillment* for the people of God. He continues to unfold His great plan of redemption until the end of the age.

---

55 A. T. Robertson, Word Pictures in the New Testament, Vol. IV, The Epistles of Paul, Baker Book House, Grand Rapids, Michigan, 1931, page 353.

CHAPTER 5
BELIEVER'S PRACTICE IN REGARDS TO THE LAW

LAW REVEALS SIN AND MAKES SIN ALIVE
7:7   EXODUS 20:17; DEUTERONOMY 5:21

Chapter 7 is the next occasion Paul uses to cite the Old Testament, here from the Decalogue (Exodus 20:17 and Deuteronomy 5:21). In this section of the epistle Paul addresses the actual working of the Law, from his experience and this applies to the ἀδελφοί in Romans 1:13 and now again in this chapter to Jew and Gentile Christians familiar with the Law.

Paul, in verse 7 uses just the beginning of Exodus 20:17 "YOU SHALL NOT COVET.". The Hebrew חמד, (chaòmad) 'covet' is elaborated by Dr. Hertz:

covet i.e. to long for the possession of anything we cannot get in an honest and legal manner, this Commandment goes to the root of all evil actions-the unholy instincts and impulses of predatory desire, which are the spring of nearly every sin against a neighbour. The man who does not covet the neighbour's goods will not bear false witness against him; he will neither rob nor murder, nor will he commit adultery. It commands self control; for every man has it in power to determine whether his desires are to master him, or he is to master his desires. Without such self control, there can be no worthy human life; it alone is the true measure of true manhood or womanhood. 'Who is strong? asks the Rabbis. 'He who controls his passions,' is their reply.[56]

LAW REVEALS SIN AND MAKES SIN ALIVE
7:7   EXODUS 20:17; DEUTERONOMY 5:21

---

56 Dr. J. H. Hertz, C. H., ed.., late Chief Rabbi of the British Empire, The Pentateuch and Haftoahs, second edition, Socini Press, London, 1970, page 300.

The Law commands obedience. Paul tells us that it remains undone and cannot save us (Galatians 2:21, *Law's second use*), the teaching is that the Law is a "tutor", Romans 7:7 provides a good example of a comprehensive use of the Law, all 3 uses, including a guide to the Christian experience.

Heinrich Meyer summarizes the first part of the illustration this way:

The Christian is not under the Mosaic law; but through his fellowship in the death of Christ he has died to the law, in order to belong to the Risen One and in this new union to lead a life consecrated to God.[57]

Paul, speaking in the first person, using his own experience as an example to all, typical to all, continues the illustration referencing an implied universal experience as an unregenerate person (7:7-13). In answering the question "Is the Law sin?", Paul uses 2 contrary to fact condition clauses, countering a false conclusion that can be drawn and emphatically presenting the deception of sin. (ἔγνων "I have known", aorist active indicative with εἰ μὴ, "If not" and ὁ νόμος ἔλεγεν, "the Law had said", imperfect active indicative with εἰ μὴ, "if not").[58] Paul immediately answers with the fact that the Law excites and reveals sin and by the specific Commandment. Contrary to a false conclusion that the Law is unholy, not righteous and not good, he concludes that the Law is a medium or an agency for sin to be exacerbated and known, Romans 7:12, "So then, the

---

[57] H. A. W. Meyer's, Critical and Exegetical Commentary on the New Testament, Romans, Vol. V., Alpha Greek Library, Winona Lake, Wisconsin, reprinted 1980. page 257.

[58] J. Harold Greenlee, A Concise Exegetical Grammar of New Testament Greek, Wm. B. Eerdmans Publishing Grand Rapids, Michigan, reprinted 1979, page 72.

Law is holy, and the commandment is holy and righteous and good."

By way of review, Paul makes the emphatic argument, giving the reason that the Law makes sin "utterly" (v. 13) sinful:

Assertion one: "I would not have come to know sin except through the Law;" contrary to the fact, he did come to know sin through the Law.

Assertion two: "If the Law had not said, 'YOU SHALL NOT COVET.'", contrary to the fact, the Law does say he did covet. By so doing, Paul is iterating his personal experience.

Richard Lenski conveys Paul's meaning:

In a simple and most natural way Paul begins to use his own experience when he makes the relation of law and sin plain in order to show we are delivered from both. No emphatic or contrasting ἐγώ is as yet needed. What is plain from the start is the fact that Paul's personal experience is offered only because it is typical of what has happened and continues to happen in the case of Christians in general. Otherwise there would be no sense in Paul's obtruding his own experience. Our individual experience may differ in minor details, but they do not differ in the essentials here sketched. It may not be just the commandment about coveting that first strikes so deeply into our consciousness; it may be some other commandment.[59]

Interestingly, Paul's own experience (Philippians 3:3-5) indicates that his expertise in Law and understanding of it surpasses all, due to the high standards his resume asserts. Why is it that he spent his young adulthood blind to the Faith? The record of his persecution of the Faith, prior to the Damascus road conversion experience is well represented in Scripture,

---

59 R. C. H. Lenski, Commentary on the New Testament, the interpretation of St. Paul's Epistle to the Romans, Hendrickson Publishing, second print March 2001, pp. 461-462.

Acts 8:3 imprisoning Christians, Acts 9:1-2, threatening murder and arrests against Christians. He readily recognized his culpability of these persecutions (1 Corinthians 15:9 and Philippians 3:5-6). The answer is in Paul's own teachings. Man is dead in trespasses and sin (Ephesians chapter 2). We die because we are sin, inflicted and infected by it (Romans 7:24).

Some Christian sects teach sinless perfectionism. Promoting a theology that asserts for the believer the idea when we sin, rather than we are sin, infected by it and doomed to the consequences of it (Romans 7:13, 21), one can only turn to Biblical teaching for escape from this deficient teaching. Luther's concept "Simul justus et peccator" is always a good reminder of our condition.

David Scaer provides insight into this dilemma of the believer, commenting on Romans 7:23:

> The problem—and it is the real problem because he can never escape it—the Christian lives in two realities. In Christ he is righteous, but in his body he sees something else at work. It is almost as if he was never converted.[60]

It is not until God's intervention into one's life the transformational regeneration and sanctification and turning of conversion takes place and then we have hope of deliverance. To be sure the Christian is promised freedom from the bondage, guilt and penalty from sin (Romans chs.6-8). But danger comes when one hears sermons touting this sinless perfection, as if, it is to be the norm for the believer, and achievable this side of the resurrection. If this teaching is adopted, pervasive harm follows with this heterodoxy. It must always be countered. Paul teaches clearly in Romans 3:10-12, this is

---

60 David Scaer, "Third Use of the Law: Resolving The Tension", 28th Annual Symposium on the Lutheran Confessions, Concordia Theological Seminary, January 2005, David P. Scaer, (PDF download on 2/02/2009).

false. How many believers are orientated in the various holiness sects and the second blessing movements and later only to reap great despair when the realization that a deficient theology had been adopted?

The best advise comes from the Apostle Paul, Philippians 3:9, "and may be found in Him, not having a righteousness of my own derived from *the* Law, but that which is through faith in Christ, the righteousness which *comes* from God on the basis of faith,"

The Christian is always to remember 1 John 2:1-2:

"My little children, I am writing these things to you so that you may not sin. And if anyone sins, we have an **Advocate** with the Father, Jesus Christ the righteous; and He Himself is the **propitiation** for our sins; and not for ours only, but also for *those of* the whole world".

Johannes Behm addressing the significance of this word, 'Advocate', παράκλητος, says:

The idea of the advocate in the OT and later Judaism is linked directly to the thought in 1 John 2:1 (Jesus Christ a paraclete of sinful Christians before the Father). Dominant is the same forensic idea of the judgment of God before which sinners are arraigned and where they need an advocate.[61]

This is inextricably linked with Paul's teaching of justification the other word John uses, propitiation, ἱλασμός, hilasmos, W. E. Vine elaborates:

---

61 Johannes Behm, ed. Gerhard Kittel, trans. Geoffrey Bromiley, (TDNT) Theological Dictionary of the New Testament Vol. V, Wm. B. Eerdmans Publishing Grand Rapids, Michigan, reprinted 1979 10th printing 1979, page 811.

The corresponding NT words are, "propitiation," 1 John 2:2; 4:10, and, Rom. 3:25; Heb. 9:5, "mercy-seat," the covering of the ark of the covenant. These describe the means (in and through the person and work of the Lord Jesus Christ, in His death on the cross by the shedding of His blood in His vicarious sacrifice for sin) by which God shows mercy to sinners.[62]

There are 2 religious systems presented to mankind. One is salvation is obtainable through a system of human works and efforts to become worthy, righteous, and good enough to merit reward, by a self defined and self originated god, in order to extricate oneself from a recognizable moral deficiency and failure. The other is from the true God and Savior, who provides the foundation and means to receive His gift, from His character, work and plan.

In line with the counter view of justification by faith and faith alone. The Roman Church has adopted the concept of purgatory. It is the, yes but, view of the work of Christ and an insult to Him. There is no Biblical basis to accept this as a tenet of faith. How does the thief on the cross that Jesus declared (Luke 23:43) "And He said to him, 'Truly I say to you, today you shall be with Me in Paradise'" fit into a purgatory scheme?

The Romanists teach souls may enter heaven after a final purging of sins for varying segments of time. Perhaps, there are some perfect Christians that enter immediately after death, but not many. It is a innovation of the heresy of salvation by human effort, works and merit.

Anyone accepting this teaching has no confidence in salvation. It is a heresy. It betrays the words of our Lord and Savior on the

---

62 W.E. Vine, Expository Dictionary of New Testament Words, Fleming H. Revell Company, Old Tappan, New Jersey, reprinted 1966, page 86.

cross, "It is finished". It derogates His work and infers it to be inadequate, insufficient and ultimately futile. As to the motivations to promote this, the reader can speculate.

Hebrews 1:3b:
"When He had made purification of sins, He sat down at the right hand of the Majesty on high,"

and Hebrew 10:12:
"but He, having offered one sacrifice for sins for all time, SAT DOWN AT THE RIGHT HAND OF GOD,"

CHAPTER 6
BRUTE FORCE DOES NOT NULLIFY THE PLAN OF GOD

WILL THE EFFORTS OF BRUTE FORCE NULLIFY THE PLAN OF GOD?
DIVINE PLAN EXCLUDES SEPARATION FROM GOD
8:36   PSALM 44:22

In chapter 8:36, the Old Testament citation that Paul uses relates to God's plan of salvation and its failure is excluded, even to the extent that brute force is used against it. Paul asserts God's accomplishment for us in verse 8:1.

Archibald Robertson, commenting on the first verse of chapter 8, summarizes this eternal benefit:

No condemnation (*ouden katakrima*). As sinners we deserved condemnation in our unregenerate state in spite of the struggle. But God offers pardon "to those in Christ Jesus (*tois en Christoôi Ieôsou*). This is Paul's gospel. The fire has burned on and around the Cross of Christ. There and there alone is safety. Those in Christ Jesus can lead the consecrated, the crucified, the baptized life.[63]

He goes on to say, in verse 36: "Just as it is written, But for Your sake we are killed all day long; We are considered as sheep to be slaughtered" is a direct quote of Psalm 44:22 "FOR YOUR SAKE WE ARE BEING PUT TO DEATH ALL DAY LONG; WE WERE CONSIDERED AS SHEEP TO BE SLAUGHTERED." Paul states that his experience, the Apostles and ongoing with Christians is that of continuous martyrdom (1 Corinthians 15:31-32).

---

[63] A. T. Robertson, Word Pictures in the New Testament, Vol. IV, The Epistles of Paul, Baker Book House, Grand Rapids, Michigan, 1931, page 372.

Considering the great persecution coming to the church in Rome after the year 64 A.D. and Paul's experiences recounted in Acts, Heinrich Meyer makes these insights:

> By way of scriptural proof for the most extreme element mentioned, for ἡ μάχαιρα, Paul quotes a passage, in accordance with which even the slaying sword has here its place already prophetically indicated beforehand. In Ps. 43:24 (quoted exactly from the LXX.), where the historical meaning refers to the daily massacres of Jews in the time of the Psalmist (in an age after the exile, but not so late as the Maccabean), he recognises a type of the analogous fate awaiting the Christian people of God, as their sacred-historic destiny.[64]

The *historical* Psalm, probably from the time of journey to the Babylonian captivity[65], (LXX Psalm 43, MT Psalm 44).[66] In verses 1-8 express anticipation for future faithfulness of the Lord in their current suffering, in verses 9-16 expresses lament and complaint and the current suffering of God's people at the hands of their enemies, recounting God's historical deliverance, in verses 17-19 praying and reasserting their faithfulness and in verses 20-26, appeal to a seemingly silent God for deliverance. Like the use of Habakkuk in chapter one, the Old Testament context shows a contemporary experience of God's people, and a hope in the future deliverance. This is very much like what the people of God experience in this day and age. The eschatological culmination of faith, while experiencing current malaise and suffering on earth. Paul reiterates this theme many times, particularly in 1 Corinthians 2:8-9, as it relates to the

---

64 H. A. W. Meyer's, Critical and Exegetical Commentary on the New Testament, Romans, Vol. V., Alpha Greek Library, Winona Lake Wisconsin, reprinted 1980, page 342.
65 F. Delitzsch, trans. Francis Bolton, Commentary on the Old Testament Vol. V, Psalms, second section, Wm. B. Eerdmans Publishing Grand Rapids, Michigan, reprinted 1981, second Volume, page 55.
66 The Septuagint (LXX) and Masoretic text (MT) vary in numbering the Psalms, see Appendix II.

historical record of Christ's sufferings and the future benefits for those in the faith. Here also, in verses 8:36-37, the familiar καθὼς γέγραπται (as it has been written) is used. This Old Testament usage by Paul is *historic* and *prophetic* in that, it speaks of future deliverance from current suffering of the Lord's people in all ages, but particularly the Church Age.

Franz Delitzsch comments on the same theme:

Paul, in Rom 8:36, transfers this utterance to the sufferings of the New Testament church borne in witnessing for the truth, or I should rather say he considers it as a divine utterance corresponding as it were prophetically to the sufferings of the New Testament church, and by anticipation, coined concerning it and for its use, inasmuch as he cites it with the words καθὼς γέγραπται.[67]

Persecution of God's people started long ago (Hebrews 11:32-38) before the Christian era, Moses, Noah and Daniel give testimony to this. For the past 20 centuries, Christian persecution has become commonplace. The Roman Epistle is written a few years prior to the Neronian persecution of 64 A.D. In addition to the events detailed in Acts, a plethora of sources can be readily found detailing the historical records.[68] The widely distributed and renown work of John *Foxe, Actes and Monuments*, popularly known as *Foxe's Book of Martyrs*, coming out of Reformation era England should be standard reading material for any serious person of the Christian Faith. The details of Christian martyrdom are presented. It is widely

---

67 F. Delitzsch, trans. Francis Bolton, Commentary on the Old Testament Vol. V., Psalms, second section, Wm. B. Eerdmans Publishing Grand Rapids, Michigan, reprinted 1981, second Volume, page 71.
68 "Persecution of Christians", Wikipedia, Wikimedia Foundation, last edited, 13 June 2020, https://en.wikipedia.org/wiki/Persecution_of_Christians#By_Christians_both_during_and_after_the_Protestant_Reformation.

distributed and easily found in print and website and electronic editions.[69]

So then, this passage, Romans 8:36, is like Paul's first use of the Old Testament in chapter one. The element of *history* and *prophecy* accompanies its use, recalling former deliverance and present trouble and foretelling the Apostolic persecution and all future persecutions of the Church from their legacy.

---

69 John Foxe, B o o k s F o r T h e A g e s, AGES Software • Albany, OR USA, Hartland Publications • Rapidan, VA USAVersion 1.0 © 1997.

CHAPTER 7
ELECTION AS EXPLANATION OF ISRAEL'S UNBELIEF

NOT ALL ARE ISRAEL FROM ISRAEL, THERE ARE 2 ISRAELS
LINEAL CORPOREAL DESCENT NOT THE DETERMINER
CHILDREN OF PROMISE ARE DESCENDANTS
9:7   GENESIS 21:12

THE ONE WHO CALLS DETERMINES CHOICE OF DESCENDANT
9:9   GENESIS 18:10
9:12   GENESIS 25:23
9:13   MALACHI 1:2FF.

OBJECTIONS TO GOD'S ELECTION ANSWERED
9:15   EXODUS 33:19
9:17   EXODUS 9:16

HOSEA'S PROPHECY
9:25   HOSEA 2:23
9:26   HOSEA 1:10

SCRIPTURAL PROOF OF ELECTION OF REMNANT
9:27   ISAIAH 10:22; GENESIS 22:17; HOSEA 1:10
9:28   ISAIAH 10:23
9:29   ISAIAH 1:9

ISAIAH'S PROPHECY
9:33   ISAIAH 28:16; [ISAIAH 8:14]

Romans chapter 9 has 12 Old Testament references. The extent to which Paul is distressed over the unbelief of the nation of Israel is expressed in verse 3, "For I could wish that I myself were accursed, *separated* from Christ for the sake of my brethren, my kinsmen according to the flesh".

The key word in Romans 9:3, accursed (ἀνάθεμα, anathema), this "is a supreme of the readiness of Paul for redemptive self-sacrifice for the people which excludes itself from the divine revelation of salvation (Exodus 32:32)".[70] Paul having the same sentiment as Moses. The word used in Exodus 32:32, מָחָה, *maw-khaw'*, wipe out, erase, blot out (figuratively) from the book of life.

Karl Keil and Franz Delitzsch comment on this blotting out words of Moses:

The book which Jehovah has written is the book of life, or of the living (Ps 69:29; Dan 12:1). This expression is founded upon the custom of writing the names of the burgesses of a town or country in a burgess-list, whereby they are recognised as natives of the country, or citizens of the city, and all the privileges of citizenship are secured to them. The book of life contains the list of the righteous (Ps 69:29), and ensures to those whose names are written there, life before God, first in the earthly kingdom of God, and then eternal life also, according to the knowledge of salvation, which keeps pace with the progress of divine revelation, e.g., in the New Testament, where the heirs of eternal life are found written in the book of life (Phil 4:3; Rev 3:5; 13:8, etc.),—an advance for which the way was already prepared by Isa 4:3 and Dan 12:1. To blot out of Jehovah's book, therefore, is to cut off from fellowship with the living God, or from the kingdom of those who live before God, and to deliver over to death. As a true mediator of his people, Moses was ready to stake his own life for the deliverance of the nation, and not to live before God himself, if Jehovah did not forgive the people their sin. These words of Moses were the strongest expression of devoted, self-sacrificing love. And they were just as deep and true as the wish expressed by the Apostle

---

70 Grundmann, Walter, ed. Gerhard Kittel, trans. Geoffrey Bromiley, (TDNT) Theological Dictionary of the New Testament Vol. I, Wm. B. Eerdmans Publishing Grand Rapids, Michigan, reprinted 1979 10th printing 1979, page 355.

Paul in Rom 9:3, that he might be accursed from Christ for the sake of his brethren according to the flesh.[71]

This same analogy is read at the end of the Bible, Revelation 22:19.

Frederic Godet describes Paul's sentiment:

He would consent, if it were possible, to fall back again for ever into the state of condemnation in which he lived before his conversion, if by the sacrifice of his salvation he could bring about the conversion of his people Israel.[72]

NOT ALL ARE ISRAEL FROM ISRAEL, THERE ARE 2 ISRAELS
LINEAL CORPOREAL DESCENT NOT THE DETERMINER
CHILDREN OF PROMISE ARE DESCENDANTS
9:7   GENESIS 21:12

THE ONE WHO CALLS DETERMINES CHOICE OF DESCENDANT
9:9   GENESIS 18:10
9:12   GENESIS 25:23
9:13   MALACHI 1:2FF.

In verses 6-13, (9:7 citing Genesis 21:12; 9:9 Genesis 18:10; 9:12 Genesis 25:23 and 9:13 Malachi 1:2ff.). These are *prophecies* and their ongoing fulfillment. Malachi's citation is coupled with God speaking in Genesis 25:23 is cited to corroborate Paul's assertions from the *historic record* of the eternal plan of God and His character and His revelation.

---

71 C. F. Keil & F. Delitzsch, trans. James Martin, Commentary on the Old Testament Vol. 1: The Pentateuch, Wm. B. Eerdmans Publishing Grand Rapids, Michigan, reprinted 1982, page 231.
72 Frederic Godet, St Paul's Epistle to the Roman Theological Library. trans. A. Cusin, new series., Vol. II, Edinburgh: T & T Clark, 38 George Street. 1881, page 134.

With these as a foundation, Paul begins his explanation of Israel's unbelief. His elaboration is that election is the explanation. The Christian doctrine of election does not eliminate human culpability for unbelief. The history of Israel and the human race clearly indicate this. He begins by pointing to Genesis 21:12 (LXX), in verse 7, that proves his point with this first reason, that physical descendency is not the determining factor of one's spiritual inheritance. The second reason he cites, in verse 9, citing Genesis 18:10 (LXX), children of the promise are descendants. The third reason he gives is that, the One who calls determines choice of descendant. Starting with verse 11, Paul states that the choice is not simply a result of human activity and history.

James Denney points out and comments on the phrase (Romans 9:11) stated literally, "not yet for having been born nor having done":

μήπω γὰρ γεννηθέντων μηδὲ πραξάντων: "the conditional negatives (μήπω, μηδὲ) represent the circumstances not as mere facts of history, but as conditions entering into God's counsel and plan. The time of the prediction was thus chosen, in order to make it clear that He Who calls men to be heirs of His salvation makes free choice of whom He will, unfettered by any claims of birth or merit" (Gifford).[73]

God's will is not dependent on the twins not being born and not doing anything good or bad. We have difficulty with this concept. God transcends the temporal world we live in. We think sequentially and are bound by time and space. The Scripture clearly teaches that there is much beyond our capacity to comprehend. Predestination is according to His purpose and according to the counsel of His will (Ephesians

---

73 James Denney, ed. W. Robertson Nicoll, The Expositor's Greek Testament, Vol. II, Wm. B. Eerdmans Publishing Grand Rapids, Michigan, reprinted 1979, page 661.

1:11). God's will is all comprehensive, all things are in His will, the secret and revealed (Deuteronomy 29:29). History and the Scripture demonstrate that it is the One who calls determines the choice of the descendants.

The parallels of Genesis 25:23 (2 individuals and nations: Jacob-Israel and Esau-Edom) and Malachi 1:2ff., cited by Paul further prove his point.

James Denney further states:

> He is obviously thinking of Jacob and Esau as individuals, whose own relation to God's promise and inheritance (involving no doubt that of their posterity) was determined by God before they were born or had done either good or ill. On the other hand, it would not be right to say that Paul here refers the eternal salvation or perdition of individuals to an absolute decree of God which has no relation to what they are or do, but rests simply on His inscrutable will. He is engaged in precluding the idea that man can have claims of right against God, and with it the idea that the exclusion of the mass of Israel from the Messiah's kingdom convicts God of breach of faith toward the children of Abraham; and this He can do quite effectually, on the lines indicated, without consciously facing this tremendous hypothesis.[74]

It helps us to think that Paul is speaking of 2 Israels. Frederic Godet explains:

> We must beware of destroying in this place the significant relation between the first and second *Israel*. The word is used both times collectively, and yet in two different applications. *They who are of Israel* denote all the members of the nation at a given moment, as descendants of the preceding generation. By the first words : are *not Israel*, Paul signalizes among the nation taken *en masse,* thus understood a *true* Israel, that elect people, that *holy remnant,* which is constantly spoken of *in* the O. T., and to which alone the decree of

---

[74] Ibid.

election refers, so that rejection may apply to the mass of *those who are of Israel,* without compromising the election of the *true Israel*.[75]

As a point of interest, the Old Testament says in 2 Samuel 8:13-14 "So David made a name *for himself* when he returned from killing 18,000 Arameans (Some mss read *Edom)* in the Valley of Salt. He put garrisons in Edom. In all Edom he put garrisons, and all the Edomites became servants to David. And the LORD helped David wherever he went." Viewing this passage from a national perspective sees this as a *fulfilled prophecy.* David out of Israel and Edom out of Esau. The defeated (older) became the bond slave to the younger. (Romans 9:12 quoting Genesis 25:23), Romans 9:13, Paul asserts election from Malachi 1:2f.

Paul however, makes this an individual argument for election of individuals as he continues on. This two Israel concept is not unlike what is seen in the churches today. It would be presumptuous to think that all individuals that attend a church service are believers, regenerate people, Romans 9:6, "For they are not all Israel who are *descended* from Israel;" and not all church goers and descendants of Christian parents are Christians. Common experience informs otherwise. This is similar to the concept of the visible and invisible church. (cf. Matthew 7:21-27; Matthew 13:24-30; Matthew 24:29-51)

As James Denney comments:

This is merely an application of our Lord's words, That which is born of the flesh is flesh. It is not what we get from our fathers and mothers that ensures our place in the family of God.[76]

---

75 Frederic Godet, St Paul's Epistle to the Roman Theological Library. trans. A.Cusin, new series., Vol. II, Edinburgh: T & T Clark, 38 George Street. 1881, page 145.
76 James Denney, ed. W. Robertson Nicoll, The Expositor's Greek Testament, Vol. II, Wm. B. Eerdmans Publishing Grand Rapids, Michigan, reprinted

This idea of election becomes imbalanced in anyone's mind and objectionable when human culpability for sin and disbelief is removed. This concept is objectionable then and now. Paul continues to access the Old Testament to demonstrate his point. God's sovereign purpose in election is Paul's theme in presentation here. He is addressing the national unbelief of Israel and in other places in his epistles and individual belief or unbelief. Israel's history is in view and how they rejected the Messiah in Paul's day until now. In John's gospel Jesus presents both sides of the issue. In John 5:40, he tells the Jews that they are unwilling to come, that do not believe Moses and the Scripture, yet they don't come unless drawn (John 6:44).

Marvin Vincent says this as to the significance of the word for drawn as it relates to election:

Draw (ἑλκύσῃ)
Two words for *drawing* are found in the New Testament, Σύρω and ἑλκύω. The distinction is not habitually observed, and the meanings often overlap. Σύρω is originally to *drag* or *trail* along, as a garment or torn slippers. Both words are used of haling to justice. (See Acts 8:3; 17:6; 16:19) In Acts 14:19, σύρω, of dragging Paul's senseless body out of the city at Lystra. In John 21:6, 8, 11, both words of drawing the net. In John 18:10, ἑλκύω, of drawing Peter's sword. One distinction, however, is observed: σύρω is never used of Christ's attraction of men. See 6:44; 12:32. ʾΕλκύω occurs only once outside of John's writings (Acts 16:19). Luther says on this passage: "The drawing is not like that of the executioner, who draws the thief up the ladder to the gallows; but it is a gracious allurement, such as that of the man whom everybody loves, and to whom everybody willingly goes."[77]

1979, page 659.
77 Marvin R. Vincent, Vincent's Word Studies, Vol 2., the Writings of John: The Gospel, The Epistles, The Apocalypse, Parsons Technology, Inc., Hiawatha, Iowa , electronic edition step files copyright © 1998.

Apart from the regenerating work of the Holy Spirit no one believes nor comes. It is the proclamation of the Word of God that brings people to Christ's life (Romans 10:8-9). These quotations (9:12-13) are all *fulfilled prophecy* and epitomize election.

OBJECTIONS TO GOD'S ELECTION ANSWERED
9:15   EXODUS 33:19
9:17   EXODUS 9:16

Objections answered have to do with assailing the fairness and justice of God in election. The first answer responds to the anticipated question that God is unrighteous. Paul is asserting that it is God's prerogative in expressing mercy (9:14-18). The first citation (verse 15) is from Exodus 33:19 (LXX). God is speaking words of assurance to Moses granting his request for continued Divine presence.

Heinrich Meyer comments on the objection to God's mercy:

In the original text it is an assurance by God to Moses of His favour now directly extended towards him, but expressed in the form of a divine axiom. Hence Paul, following the LXX., was justified in employing the passage as a scriptural statement of the general proposition: God's mercy, in respect of the persons concerned, whose lot it should be to experience it, lets itself be determined solely by His own free will of grace: "I will have mercy upon whosoever is the object of my mercy;" so that I am therefore in this matter dependent on nothing external to myself. This is the sovereignty of the divine compassionating will. Observe that the future denotes the actual compassion, fulfilling itself in point of fact, which God promises to show to the persons concerned, towards whom He stands in the mental relation (ἐλεῶ, present) of pity.[78]

---

78 H. A. W. Meyer's, Critical and Exegetical Commentary on the New Testament, Romans, Vol. V., Alpha Greek Library, Winona Lake Wisconsin,

One of the perfections of God is His goodness. As a general definition of mercy, one of the ways He expresses His goodness - it is the expression of the goodness of God shown to those in misery or distress irrespective of what they deserve. Psalm 136:1, "Give thanks to the LORD, for He is good". The need for the righteousness of God, a teaching presented by Paul assiduously, indicates that mankind cannot attain it on their own. It is solely dependent on His sovereign will. So how can the fairness and justice of God be attacked based on giving mercy according to His will, man unable to lay any claim to it?

The next citation, addressing Pharaoh (verse 17), "FOR THIS VERY PURPOSE I RAISED YOU UP, TO DEMONSTRATE MY POWER IN YOU, AND THAT MY NAME MIGHT BE PROCLAIMED THROUGHOUT THE WHOLE EARTH." Paul, from Exodus 9:16 varies the LXX and Hebrew but captures the meaning. He is pointing to the sovereignty of God in history to accomplish His purpose of salvation.

The Hebrew text has הֶעֱמַדְתִּיךָ (heemadticha, I have raised you up), (עָמַד root, *aw-mad'* here the Hithpael perfect verb is used and means to *cause* to stand or maintain (opp. overthrow)[79]. The context is God pointing out to Pharaoh that he could be cut off (Exodus 9:15), so in opposition "I have maintained you". Exodus 9:16 "But, indeed, for this reason I have allowed you to remain, in order to show you My power and in order to proclaim My name through all the earth." The LXX translates "I allowed you to remain", or "I caused you to subsist" using

---

reprinted 1980, page 373.
79 Francis Brown, S. R. Driver, Charles Briggs, (NBDBG) trans., Edward Robinson, The New Brown Driver Briggs Gesenius Hebrew Aramaic English Lexicon, Associated Publishers and Authors, Inc., Lafayette, Indiana, 1980, page 764.

διετηρήθης, "you have been *preserved*"[80], or "you were carefully kept".

The Scripture (v. 17 λέγει γὰρ ἡ γραφὴ, for the scripture says) always speaks authoritatively, because God speaks through His Word. It is not merely the words of a man, or something contained in Scripture (Galatians 3:8, 22). This personification, "scripture says", is seen of Scripture as a whole.[81] Paul is giving another aspect of his answer. Just as much the giving and demonstration of mercy is solely dependent on God, so is His purpose in His giving and demonstrating wrath. Pharaoh, King of Egypt, the hardened man would not repent. The account shows how he survives the plagues, pestilence, hail, fire and thunder, for a time, but his people and their animals and some agriculture do not. Psalm 136:15 indicates Pharaoh met his ultimate demise. God's purpose in preserving Israel preserves the coming Messiah that will save the whole world through the gospel. Paul concludes from the *historical* record that objection to God being unrighteous does not stand and is *prophetic*. Mercy is outside of mankind and dependent on God alone and wrath is the inbuilt result of human sinfulness, our culpability. As a prime example, Pharaoh. God is not unrighteous because of this.

As James Denney asserts the design of Pharaoh's purpose:

The purpose Pharaoh was designed to serve, and actually did serve, on this stage, was certainly not his own; as certainly it was God's. God's

---

[80] Sir Lancelot Brenton, Sir Lancelot C. L., The Septuagint Version: Greek and English, Septuagint version of the Old Testament, Zondervan Corporation, Grand Rapids, Michigan, 1970, page 81.
[81] Gottlob Schrenk, ed. Gerhard Kittel, trans. Geoffrey Bromiley, (TDNT) Theological Dictionary of the New Testament Vol. I, Wm. B. Eerdmans Publishing Grand Rapids, Michigan, reprinted 1979 10th printing 1979, pp. 753-754.

power was shown in the penal miracles by which Pharaoh and Egypt were visited, and his name is proclaimed to this day wherever the story of the Exodus is told.[82]

The second anticipated objection is that of denying human culpability (9:19-24). How can mankind be culpable if God in election determines the outcome? Paul answers that this does not stand, and mankind is not competent even to discuss it (v.20).

Frederic Godet asserts our incompetence:

We acknowledge that in vv. 19 and 20 Paul pleads solely man's incompetency to discuss the dealings of God.[83]

As then is true now. Mankind questions God as if He must conform to our line of thinking. Man is depraved (Romans 1:28-32). How can eternity be judged by the temporal? How can the creature judge the Creator? Systematic theology takes the Scripture and endeavors to categorize the character and attributes of God. In this discussion about questioning God, it must be stated that the God of the Christian Scriptures has the quality of aseity and omnipotence - He is uncaused, independent, self-sufficient (Exodus 3:14). He exists in and of Himself. Mankind is not in a position to assail His character. Paul is putting the question in its rightful place that the creature not in a place to judge the Creator.

HOSEA'S PROPHECY
9:25   HOSEA 2:23

---

[82] James Denney, ed. W. Robertson Nicoll, The Expositor's Greek Testament, Vol. II, Wm. B. Eerdmans Publishing Grand Rapids, Michigan, reprinted 1979 page 662.
[83] Frederic Godet, St Paul's Epistle to the Roman Theological Library. trans. A. Cusin, new series., Vol. II, Edinburgh: T & T Clark, 38 George Street. 1881, page 162.

9:26 HOSEA 1:10

The simile continues to establish the doctrine of election and states that God saves some out of the lump of clay that is humanity in the illustration. God's wrath is the natural outcome of human sin. A man cannot save himself. So how can the outcome, destruction or mercy make God culpable and man exonerated? He references Hosea the prophet to prove his point Romans 9:25-26. He points to the prophesy of the calling and non exclusion of the Gentiles to be objects of mercy. The current and continuing of God's election gives prima facie exhibition from the *prophecy* of Hosea (Hosea 2:23 אָמַר, aòmar, God speaking; 1:10) as being fulfilled and would be ongoing like Habakkuk 2:4 in Paul's citation in Romans 1:17, as more Gentiles are called. Jesus says, (John 10:16) "I have other sheep, which are not of this fold; I must bring them also, and they will hear My voice; and they will become one flock *with* one shepherd."

SCRIPTURAL PROOF OF ELECTION OF REMNANT
9:27   ISAIAH 10:22; GENESIS 22:17; HOSEA 1:10
9:28   ISAIAH 10:23
9:29   ISAIAH 1:9

The combination in 9:27 of Isaiah 10:22, Genesis 22:17, Hosea 1:10 presented by Paul as evidence of God's election. In verse 28, Isaiah 10:23 is used and Isaiah 1:9 in verse 29. This use of the Old Testament passages is linking past reckoning and ongoing prophecy. Isaiah cries out, κράζει (verse 27), is in the context of promised judgment upon Israel and its swift and certain execution (verse 28). The prior mention of Sodom and Gomorrah (Romans 9:29) make this clear and is always used to emphasize judgment in the New Testament (Matthew 10:15; 11:23, Luke 10:12; 17:29, Romans 9:29, 2 Peter 2:6, Jude 1:7, Revelation 11:8). Sadly, from the great multitude of Israel only a small portion are saved, which is also true of the human race

(Matthew 7:13-14). This is not unprecedented. The Jews wandered in the wilderness 40 years (Joshua 5:6) and only Caleb and Joshua entered the promised land, even Moses was excluded. Only Noah and his family were saved from the flood. Jesus said in Matthew 7:13-14, "Enter through the narrow gate; for the gate is wide and the way is broad that leads to destruction, and there are many who enter through it. For the gate is small and the way is narrow that leads to life, and there are few who find it."

Just as Paul's argument comes from Hosea's and Isaiah's *prophecy* he continues to reiterate from *prophecy* and past *historical record* that only a remnant of the Jews are saved.

ISAIAH'S PROPHECY
9:33   ISAIAH 28:16; [ISAIAH 8:14]

The Jews and the Gentiles are compared once again, 9:30-33. The system of works the Jews used to obtain righteousness fails because God's righteousness can only be obtained through faith (verse 32). The Gentiles not using that system obtain that righteousness.

Frederic Godet writes about this dichotomy:

The question: *What shall we say then?* has in the present case peculiar gravity : "The explanation of the fact not being found by saying, God has annulled His word; what, then, is the solution of the enigma ?" Thus, after setting aside the false solution, Paul invites his reader to seek with him the true one; and this solution he expresses in ver. 31 in a declaration of painful solemnity, after prefacing it in ver. 30 with a saying relating to the lot of the Gentiles. While the latter have obtained what they sought not, the Jews have missed what they sought; the most poignant irony in the whole of history.[84]

Romans 9:33, "just as it is written, 'Behold, I lay in Zion a stone of stumbling and a rock of offense, And he who believes in Him will not be disappointed.'"

Figurative language used here from the Hebrew and LXX by Paul. Paul is blending Isaiah 28:16, the stone laid in Zion with Isaiah 8:14, the stumbling stone. His argument appeals to the prophet Isaiah. The stumbling stone and rock of offense comes from Isaiah 8:14.

Gustav Stahlin remarks:

By the fusion of the two verses Scripture itself becomes the crown witness for the twofold meaning of the stone, i.e., the twofold operation of Jesus. He who is placed there for faith Himself becomes an '"obstacle to faith". Hence He who is appointed for salvation can also be a "cause of perdition".[85]

The Jews expected the Messiah to bring political deliverance and Kingdom restoration. Even the Apostles had this view in mind after the resurrection and before Pentecost (Acts 1:6). Jesus' triumphal entry into Jerusalem recorded in Matthew chapter 21 indicates this. The Jewish leaders were displeased with an enthusiastic reception by the crowd (Matthew 21:15). Opinions change quickly when persuasion is introduced, so within a week the mob of angry Jews, led by the leadership of

---

84 Frederic Godet, St Paul's Epistle to the Roman Theological Library. trans. A. Cusin, new series., Vol. II, Edinburgh: T & T Clark, 38 George Street. 1881, page 180.
85 Gustav Stahlin, ed. Gerhard Kittel, trans. Geoffrey Bromiley, (TDNT) Theological Dictionary of the New Testament Vol. VII, Wm. B. Eerdmans Publishing Grand Rapids, Michigan, reprinted 1979 10th printing 1979, page 352.

the religious community were soon crying for His crucifixion (Matthew 27:20). It would not be a distortion of any inference to think that many of these were the same persons that welcomed Jesus to Jerusalem. They were there for the Passover festival. Included in those present were Gentiles who had been converted to Judaism. Some of this mob may have believed later on.

Nothing has changed over the centuries, mankind is the same whether religious or not. This does not matter to Paul's gospel, the "righteous man shall live by faith". Jesus presents a problem to all those who do not believe the gospel. He is offensive. The message of the gospel commands men to repent and believe (Acts 3:19) in a person who is conceived of a virgin. This is contrary to a natural man's fallen nature and reasoning. This evolves into a concept of Jesus to be a great teacher or religious leader or prophet, like many others in the world of religions. Furthermore, the gospel states that this ordinary man (Isaiah 53) died an ignominious death about twenty centuries ago. In this death, He bears and satisfies the penalty due God for our sin because we are unable to satisfy God's requirement (Romans 5:6). The requirement is not an option, there is no other way to God. All mankind stands in judgment under this standard for which God has furnished proof (Acts 17:31). Rejection brings wrath, belief brings life (John 3:36). Believers are free from our sins because Christ Jesus took our place.

Handley Carr Glyn Moule summarizes:

In this prophetic passage St Paul is led to find (1) a prediction of Israel's stumbling at the truth of Christ our Justification, and thus to reassure minds disquieted by the sight of Israel's unbelief; (2) a proclamation of Faith (reposed on Christ) as the means of salvation.[86]

And James Denney on Romans 9:33 states:

Some stumble over Him (as the Jews, for the reasons just given); others build on Him and find Him a sure foundation, or (without a figure) put their trust in Him and are not put to shame. Cf. Psalm 118:22, Matthew 21:42, 1 Corinthians 3:11, Acts 4:12, Ephesians 2:20.[87]

Paul points to *prophecy* and the *historical record* of God's sovereignty and intervention into human history to prove his assertions. He points out that the Lord's plans cannot be thwarted or frustrated by sinful men and their history.

---

86 H. C. G. Moule, Studies in Romans, Kregel Publications, Grand Rapids, Michigan, reprinted 1982, page 178.
87 James Denney, ed. W. Robertson Nicoll, The Expositor's Greek Testament, Vol. II, Wm. B. Eerdmans Publishing Grand Rapids, Michigan, reprinted 1979, page 668.

Chapter 8
Rejection of Israel

RIGHTEOUSNESS BASED ON FAITH IS GOD'S WORK
10:6 DEUTERONOMY 30:12
10:7 DEUTERONOMY 30:13
10:8 DEUTERONOMY 30:14

RIGHTEOUSNESS BASED ON FAITH IS INDEMNIFIED
AND UNIVERSALLY AVAILABLE
10:11 ISAIAH 28:16
10:13 JOEL 2:32

RIGHTEOUSNESS BASED ON FAITH IS A SANCTIONED AND
AUTHORIZED PROCLAMATION
10:15 ISAIAH 52:7

THE GOSPEL PROCLAMATION CAN BE IGNORED
10:16 ISAIAH 53:1
10:18 PSALM 19:4

NEVERTHELESS THE GOSPEL PROCLAMATION IS HEARD BY
THE CALLING OF THE GENTILES
10:19 DEUTERONOMY 32:21
10:20 ISAIAH 65:1

DISOBEDIENCE AND OBSTINANCE ARE RESULTS OF IGNORING
10:21 ISAIAH 65:2

The next citations in Romans 10:6-8 of the Pentateuch by the Apostle must be seen consistent with the theme he has been presenting. The contrast between the Jews and their system of works as a means of obtaining righteousness and the righteousness that comes by faith. The passage he uses is from Deuteronomy 30:12-14 address the religion that God intends for His people from the very beginning accessibility to the one true God by faith. Deuteronomy demonstrates God's abundant mercy as it is the second giving of the Law. Paul contrasts doing with believing.

The words of Deuteronomy 30:11, "not too difficult for you, nor is it out of reach", parallels Jesus' words speaking of "His light yoke and easy burden". God's religion is not to be made a rigid system of execution of rules implemented and mistaken by men, that no one will be able to keep anyway because of the fallen nature, but rather faith that the Lord provides is the means for obtaining deliverance. Man cannot extricate himself from this condition with a self originated obligatory religious system. The attempt to try, always brings despair and failure because of sin. It is the provision that God gives that brings deliverance (Galatians 2:21).

What Paul is describing here by using Moses's words (Deuteronomy 30:12-14) corroborates Paul's presentation of the gospel. God is the deliverer. He sent his Son into this world to accomplish salvation for all men by His death and resurrection. Mankind cannot do it. Paul personifies faith and writes, Romans 10:6-8 ... faith speaks as follows: "DO NOT SAY IN YOUR HEART, 'WHO WILL ASCEND INTO HEAVEN?' (that is, to bring Christ down), or 'WHO WILL DESCEND INTO THE ABYSS?' (that is, to bring Christ up from the dead). "THE WORD IS NEAR YOU, in your mouth and in your heart"—that is, the word of faith which we are preaching,". Paul is saying and using Moses' words and *prophecy*, that what the Jews are trying to do, self justification cannot be done.

S. R. Driver says of the 2 figures employed by Moses in this passage:

it is not in heaven,- in an inaccessible height; which none can scale; *neither is it beyond the sea* in some distant region which none can visit, for the purpose of fetching it thence, and bringing it to Israel's knowledge.-14. *But the word is very nigh to thee, in thy mouth and in thy heart that thou mayest do it*] it has been brought so near to thee- viz. By prophets and other teachers, and especially in the discourses of Dt. That thou canst talk of its familiarity with thy lips (cf. 6:7 11:19) and mediate upon it in thy heart (cf. 6:6 11;18) thou art consequently placed in a position for giving it practical effect.[88]

It is interesting to note that Paul does not quote exactly from the LXX or the MT in this place, but the Targum. Instead, although referencing the Mosaic prophecy and uses ἀναβαίνω (to ascend) literally corresponding to Moses words, 'Deuteronomy 30:12, 'go up to heaven", with καταβαίνω (to descend into the abyss) conceptually corresponding to the Deuteronomy 30:13, 'beyond the sea'.

Handley Carr Glyn Moule provides this insight of verse 7:

Who shall descend, &c.] The Heb. has "Who shall go over (or on) the sea?"; the LXX., "to the other side of the sea?" St Paul takes the sea, as surely Moses took it, to be the antithesis of "heaven"—the "great deep;" and thus the idea is of exploring depth rather than breadth. The Jerusalem Targum on Deuteronomy has a remarkable paraphrase: "Neither is the law beyond the great sea, that thou shouldest say, O that we had one like Jonah the prophet, to descend into the depths of the sea, and bring it to us!" (Etheridge's Translation.) To Moses, sky and sea were suggestive of heights and depths of supernatural mystery. St Paul finds in this use of them the latent truth of the special Height of Christ's pre-existent majesty and the special Depth of His entrance at death into the world of souls; and so sees here an inspired declaration that this His Descent and Ascent were so "finished" as to make the means of salvation a prepared and present reality to the believing soul, which is asked (thanks to Divine mercy) not to

---

88 S. R. Driver, A Critical and Exegetical Commentary on Deuteronomy, Charles Scribner and Sons, 1902, page 331.

elaborate, but to accept, the "righteousness of God" in the Incarnate and Risen Christ.[89]

This Old Testament use here (Romans 10:6-8), is *fulfilled prophecy* of how the gospel is mistaken (Romans 10:5) then and now, not only among the Jews but of all men. Paul has thus far pointed out that salvation is not by works. This teaching is to be understood as Divine monergism, it is the theological term that finds its roots in the Pelagian controversy of about A. D. 400, ... "God is the sole agent in man's salvation."[90] The Jews developed a system of merits that they thought would justify them before God. They also believed that lineal corporeal descent granted them favor. Paul has already taught that descent or works do not justify. Faith is the universal means that God has made for all men to lay hold of His gift.

This erroneous thinking is still common among all men and seen among church goers. There are 2 ways of salvation taught in the sphere of the Christian Church. The true way, monergism, vicarious atonement and justification through faith in Christ only, Christ plus nothing. The wrong way, self justification and faith in one's own works via natural man's abilities, Christ plus your works. This implies synergism. Until individuals understand this, they have a deficient faith. It is also consistent from the testimony of Scripture that this is seen. It started with Cain. In Genesis chapter 4, the 2 brothers brought sacrifices. The faith in Hebrews 11:4, is simple to

---

89 H. C. G. Moule, Studies in Romans, Kregel Publications, Grand Rapids, Michigan, reprinted 19892, page 181. He is referencing, The Targum of Jonathan Ben Uzziel On the Pentateuch With The Fragments of the Jerusalem Targum From the Chaldee, By J . W. Etheridge, M.A.1862, pp. 650-655, Ch.29-30.
90 Philip Edgcumbe Hughes, Baker's Dictionary of Theology, eds., Everett Harrison, Geoffrey Bromiley, Carl Henry, Baker Book House, Grand Rapids, Michigan, 1978, page 510.

understand. Abel had faith and Cain did not, explaining the rejection of Cain's offering in Genesis chapter 4. The "certain persons have crept in unnoticed' in Jude's Epistle are directly linked to the "way of Cain". Much can be said regarding attitudes and expressions of the corruption of the souls of "certain men have crept in", but clearly inferred by Jude is that they are not persons of faith. They are not justified, i.e., the opposite of those who receive the benefits of life, death and resurrection of the only Lord and Savior. The Old Testament saints receive the benefit of the future work of Christ just as the New Testament saints receive the benefits of the past work of Christ. When churchgoers get this wrong, 2 inferences can be made, first, they have been taught wrongly and do not self correct or secondly, they are not Christians. It has been troubling to hear, Sunday school lessons that erroneously assert Abel's sacrifice is received and Cain's is not, because Abel brought his best to God and Cain did not, as if they were both of faith and you should do likewise, i.e., bring your best and work together with God for salvation.

Patrick Fairbairn in his section titled Sacrificial worship commenting on the Cain and Abel (Genesis 4 and Hebrews 11:4) account summarizes this way:

Taking this in its obvious and natural meaning, Cain is presented in our view as a child of nature, not of grace-as one obeying the impulse and direction only of reason, and rejecting the more explicit light of faith as to the kind of service he presented to his Maker. His oblation is an undoubted specimen of what man could do in his fallen state to originate proper ideas of God, and given fitting expression to these in outward acts of worship.[91]

---

91 Patrick Fairbairn. The Typology of Scripture, Zondervan Publishing House, Grand Rapids, Michigan, 1952, page 248.

Lewis Sperry Chafer also sheds light on this perspective of the Genesis chapter 4:

The wrathful attitude of Balak is a reflection of the attitude of Satan who energized him. In like manner, the evil which was condemned in Cain is not immorality, but rather the Satanic ideal of self-worthiness as a basis of divine acceptance. The blood-sacrifice of Abel, looking on to the fruits of redemption, provided a perfect relationship to God to which no fallen being could ever attain by works of personal righteousness.[92]

As W. Sanday, A. C. Headlam details the Jewish attitude derived from the system of merits they developed that Paul references:

Their own method was based on a rigid performance of legal enactments. But that has been ended in Christ. Now there is a new and a better way, one which has two characteristics ; it is based on the principle of faith, and it is universal and for all men alike, '(i) It is based on the principle of faith. Hence it is that while the old method was difficult, if not impossible, the new is easy and open to all. The old method righteousness by law, that is by the exact performance of legal rules, is aptly described by Moses when he says (Lev. xviii. 5), the man who does these things shall live, i.e. Life in all its fulness here and hereafter was to be gained by undeviating strictness of conduct ; and that condition we have seen (i. i8-iii. 20) was impossible of fulfillment.[93]

Adam Clarke comments on the same passage on self establishing righteousness:

---

92 Lewis Sperry Chafer, Systematic Theology, Vol II, Dallas Seminary Press, Dallas, Texas, 1947, page 60.
93 W. Sanday, A. C. Headlam, The International Critical Commentary, Critical and Exegetical Commentary on the Epistle to the Romans Edinburgh: T & T Clark, 1902, page 277.

The law, and a punctual observance of it, were the ground of their expectations in a future world. And as for the Messiah, they supposed his coming and kingdom related only to the temporal prosperity and grandeur of the Jewish nation, and the perpetual establishment of their law, by rescuing them out of the hands of the Gentile powers, who had greatly embarrassed and distressed their constitution. Thus they endeavored to establish their own righteousness, (Romans 10:3), salvation, or interest in God; an interest which they imagined for themselves, and which excluded men of all other nations, who they thought were in fact utterly excluded from the Divine favor and eternal life, as quite lost and hopeless.[94]

RIGHTEOUSNESS BASED ON FAITH IS INDEMNIFIED
AND UNIVERSALLY AVAILABLE
10:11   ISAIAH 28:16
10:13   JOEL 2:32

In Romans 10:11 and 13, is now focused on the only way to come to God, faith. Isaiah 28:16 and Joel 2:32 and their prophecies foretell the unfolding, unequivocal and universal way that God ordained, Romans 10:11, "For the Scripture says, 'Whoever believes in Him will not be disappointed.'" (λέγει γὰρ ἡ γραφὴ, Πᾶς ὁ πιστεύων ἐπ' αὐτῷ οὐ καταισχυνθήσεται (Kataischunoô, shall not be ashamed), Πᾶς - all, whoever, whosoever, is added by Paul to Isaiah's prophecy. It can be translated as "All the believing ones." Both the LXX[95], has "o πιστεύων, the believing one, and the MT[96], has, "הַמַּאֲמִין", (ham·ma·'ă·mîn root word אָמַן, modern English word amen,

---

94 Adam Clarke, Adam Clarke's Commentary on the New Testament, Electronic Edition STEP Files Copyright © 1999, Parsons Technology, Inc, section: Observations Extracted from Dr. Taylor.
95 Sir Lancelot Brenton, Sir Lancelot C. L., The Septuagint Version: Greek and English, Septuagint version of the Old Testament, Zondervan Corporation, Grand Rapids, Michigan, 1970, page 861.
96 Biblia Hebraica Stuttgartensia, ed., Karl Elliger, Wilhelm Rudolph et al., Deutsche Bibelstiftung, Stuttgart, Germany, 1967/77, page 715. (MT) Masoretic text.

the one believing), Paul makes it universal with this addition, πᾶς, "all", whoever, whosoever, any, everyone-who believes or all who believe.

Alfred Jepson in the TDOT makes this summary elaboration of הַמַּאֲמִין the one believing:

Thus *he'emin* contains a judgment about what deserves or does not deserve confidence. Perhaps the best paraphrases that have been suggested to convey the meaning of *he'emin* are: "to gain stability, to rely on someone, to give credence to a message or to consider it to be true, to trust in someone."[97]

As said previously and reiterated by Paul in Romans, that faith saves, the means God has provided to lay hold of His promised salvation. It is the universal means for all mankind.

As James Denney comments on the addition:

This verse proves from Scripture the main idea in the preceding, viz., that faith saves. It is a quotation from Isaiah 28:16 (see Romans 9:33) with the addition of πᾶς, to which nothing corresponds either in Hebr. or LXX. Yet oddly enough it is on this πᾶς that the rest of the Apostle's argument turns. The way of righteousness and salvation by faith, he goes on to show, is meant for all.[98]

The LXX translates Joel 2:32 from the MT, which Paul cites in Romans 10:13 this way: "και *And* ἐσται *it will be* πας *all* ος

---

97 Alfred Jepson, eds., G. Johannes Botterweck, Helmer Ringgren, trans., John T. Willis, (TDOT) Theological Dictionary of the Old Testament, Vol I, Wm. B. Eerdmans Publishing Company, Grand Rapids, Michigan, 1974, pp. 307-308.
98 James Denney, ed. W. Robertson Nicoll, The Expositor's Greek Testament, Vol. II, Wm. B. Eerdmans Publishing Grand Rapids, Michigan, reprinted 1979, pp. 671-672.

who αν *ever* επικαλέσηται *shall call upon* το *the* όνομα *name* κυρίου *of [the] LORD* σωθήσεται shall be delivered."

The universal call of the gospel that Paul begins to speak about in verses 14 and 15 is not restricted to a divided religious world, Jews and Gentiles, but is unrestricted in access by proclamation to both. Belief in the gospel makes one secure against future loss.

RIGHTEOUSNESS BASED ON FAITH IS A SANCTIONED AND
AUTHORIZED PROCLAMATION
10:15   ISAIAH 52:7

In Romans 10:15, it naturally follows that this message of salvation is designed to be heard by all. Paul quotes the Prophet Isaiah (52:7 "those who announce salvation") and the historic setting of the deliverance of the captives from Babylon. This includes the proclamation of God reigns throughout the whole earth (Isaiah 52:10) "That all the ends of the earth may see The salvation of our God", and answers his question: "πῶς (How) δὲ (now) κηρύξωσιν (shall they preach) ἐὰν (if) μὴ (not) ἀποσταλῶσιν (they are sent)? καθὼς (As) γέγραπται (it has been written): "Ὡς (How) ὡραῖοι (beautiful) οἱ (the) πόδες (feet) τῶν (of those) εὐαγγελιζομένων (proclaiming good news) ‹τὰ› (of) ἀγαθά (good things)!"

He also makes this a *fulfilled prophecy* declaring that the good news then is also the good news now and must be proclaimed, heralded as spoken as from the Lord.

Henry Alford sees fulfilled prophecy in Romans 10:15:

The Apostle is showing the necessity and dignity of the preachers of the word, which leads on to the universality of their preaching, leaving all who disobey it without excuse. He therefore cites this, as showing that their instrumentality was one recognized in the prophetic word, where their office is described and glorified. The applicability of these words to the preachers of the gospel is evident from the passage in Isaiah itself, which is spoken indeed of the return from captivity, but in that return has regard to a more glorious one under the future Redeemer. We need not therefore say that the Apostle uses Scripture words merely as expressing his own thoughts in a well known garb ;— he alleges the words as a prophetic description of the preachers of whom he is writing.[99]

This is significant for the modern church. The idea of everyone is a preacher or minister makes casual regard of the Scriptures and the tenets concerning the preaching and what Paul states here. The 2 words of significance he uses are κηρύσσω and ἀποστέλλω, to preach and to send.

The third class condition is used, fulfillment is likely but uncertain. The preaching and sending are conditions of contingency, (if) with the subjunctive mood.[100] Gerhard Friedrich makes salient points as to this proclamation:[101]

1. The hearing demands faith (1 Corinthians 2:4).
2. The listening demands obedience, the act of obedience is effected by God's Word (Romans 10:8).
3. Faith and proclamation have the same content (1 Corinthians 15:14).
4. To preach κηρύσσειν and to send ἀποστέλλειν are linked in the NT (Mark 3:14; Luke 4:18,43 f.; 9:2; 1 Timothy 2:7; 2 Timothy 1:11).
5. The proclamation and exposition are mutually inclusive (Luke 4:21).

---

99 Henry Alford, Alford's Greek New Testament, Vol., II, Baker Book House, Grand Rapids, Michigan, reprint 1980, page 421.
100 J. Harold Greenlee, A Concise Exegetical Grammar of New Testament Greek, Wm. B. Eerdmans Publishing Grand Rapids, Michigan, 1979, page 71.
101 Gerhard Friedrich, ed. Gerhard Kittel, trans. Geoffrey Bromiley, (TDNT) Theological Dictionary of the New Testament Vol. III, Wm. B. Eerdmans Publishing Grand Rapids, Michigan, reprinted 1979, pp. 712-713.

The resurrection is proof to all men (Acts 17:31). So where are the preachers? It has been heard and not uncommon, especially around Easter time, for pastors to tell congregants that "Jesus did not really rise from the dead, it is just symbolic. It is written to encourage us". The pastor doesn't tell the congregants that he also has an elevator that takes him down to hell after each Easter Sunday morning sermon. There are pastors, no doubt, that do not believe and apply their main efforts each week to the bulletin and not the sermon and also promoting heresy. (cf. Jude 1:4, crept in).

Unless the churches and their para-church organizations (seminaries, bible colleges and mission organizations) believe the gospel, they might as well give up and just form a mutually beneficial social group. How many pastors use the original languages in their sermon preparation and admit whatever learned in their education has been readily forgotten? In times past, it was thought that Greek and Hebrew language mastery in any Biblical education degree were mountains that ministerial candidates had to climb, apart from the assumption they are believers. For the gospel to be heard preachers must be sent. That means training, recognition, qualification and resources.

Michael J. Kruger made these insightful comments in an article from 2014 concerning ministerial candidacy attitudes, demeanor and recommendation regarding the Biblical languages and their study:[102]

1. Students should not consider Biblical languages something simply

---

102 Michael Kruger, August 18, 2014, 'You Don't Think Learning the Biblical Languages is Worth It? Think Again', retrieved from website November 27, 2020, www.michaeljkruger.com/you-dont-think-learning-the-biblical-languages-is-worth-it-think-again.

to be endured.
2. Pastoral ministry is to be a "minister of the word." This includes a serious study of the biblical text. Pastors should continue to be students. They need to be readers, thinkers, and theologians.
3. A pastor's "study" is now called the pastor's "office" (because pastors view themselves more as a CEO). It should be like going into a carpenter's shop and seeing all the tools the pastor uses, books. Pastors as ministers of the Word, keeping up with the biblical languages should be a natural part of their weekly activity.
4. Seminary students assume that the study of the languages is useless if the specifics are forgotten at a later point. This assumption, is a mistake. Intensive study of the languages during seminary still plays an enormously significant role, it helps students think textually.
5. Understanding grammar, syntax, logical flow, and sentence structure avoids certain exegetical fallacies and maintains proper interpretation of the text and preparation of a sermon (cf. Ephesians 4:11-13).

Another point needs to be made regarding ministerial qualifications and training. In this day and age there is an abundance of people interested in the Bible. This is great. The situation that this writer has observed listening to AM radio or watching television morning news show is that some of the hosts mention how "last night they went to a Bible study and prayer time". It was described as, "we read some Scripture and went around the room for everyone's input as to what this means to you", type of discussion. There was no mention of a pastor-teacher present. One can only imagine the answers and conclusions some people give and some people conclude, if this is the only genre of Bible study they are exposed to. So if the clergy persons do not adhere to a regimented study as Michael Kruger comments, why would laymen?

Once, this writer was aware in a corporate setting that fellow Christians wanted to get together at lunch time and have a Bible study and prayer time. Group members would take turns leading the group as they did sometimes in corporate meetings. It would include the same offering as the AM radio or television format. In this particular case, one of the rotating leaders was a Jehovah Witness. Apart from an evangelical opportunity to engage and refute the cult member's belief, not one in this group grasped the concept that Jehovah Witnesses have an official teaching in their organization that is patently anti-Christian and needless to say none would be prepared to engage heresy. Would any be ready to do what 1 Peter 3:15 commands? The key word in that passage is defense, ἀπολογίαν, apologia, "verbal defence, speech in defence".[103]

Another experience by this writer includes sampling a church's tract display rack and discovering Christmas tracts, that a naive church member placed. The publisher advertises their church and television ministry and it turns out the individual is an advocate of modal monarchianism[104], a revival of the ancient heresy, Sabellianism, an inadequate conception of the Trinity.[105] When was the last time the pastor viewed and audited the rack?

All this can lead to a bad outcome. Why would the New Testament contain polemic Epistles (Corinthian letters, Galatians, Colossians, Johannine letters, Jude) if there would not be a continuing infiltration by heterodoxical and heretical doctrines continuing to creep into the church?

Remember what the word of God says, Ephesians 4:11-12: "And He gave some *as* apostles, and some *as* prophets, and some *as* evangelists, and some *as* pastors and teachers, for the

---

103 Joseph Henry Thayer, translated revised and enlarged, Greek English-Lexicon of the New Testament, Harper & Brothers, New York, Cincinnati, Chicago, American Book Company, 1889, page 65.
104 William Kelly, Baker's Dictionary of Theology, Everett Harrison, ed., Baker Book House, Grand Rapids, Michigan, 1978, page 361.
105 Ibid., page 465.

equipping of the saints for the work of service, to the building up of the body of Christ".

Biblical teaching requires organization and skill and is not for everyone. The other danger comes and we are reminded by the Apostle Peter speaking about Paul's writings.

2 Peter 3:16-17: "as also in all *his* letters, speaking in them of these things, in which are some things hard to understand, which the untaught and unstable distort, as *they do* also the rest of the Scriptures, to their own destruction. You therefore, beloved, knowing this beforehand, be on your guard so that you are not carried away by the error of unprincipled men and fall from your own steadfastness,"

THE GOSPEL PROCLAMATION CAN BE IGNORED
10:16   ISAIAH 53:1
10:18   PSALM 19:4

In Romans 10:16, citing Isaiah 53:1, he summarizes the failure of Israel, unbelief of the Jews and how the publication of the gospel, just as he says of the results of election (Romans 9:27-28), produces belief and non-belief (Romans 10:16) and is *prophetic.*

The reason for unbelief and not all 'heed the good news' is as Heinrich Meyer states:

prophetic confirmation of the sad phenomenon (οὐ πάντες κ.τ.λ.), which thus, as already predicted, enters into the connection of divine destiny, and is not an accidental occurrence.[106]

---

[106] H. A. W. Meyer's, Critical and Exegetical Commentary on the New Testament, Romans, Vol. V., Alpha Greek Library, Winona Lake Wisconsin, reprinted 1980, page.414, κ.τ.λ.=και τα λοιπά = etc.

Anticipating the objection that there is no proclamation or publication of this gospel, Paul asserts that it has gone out (10:18) to the whole world just as the works and word of God are declared by King David in Psalm 19:4, declaring wisdom expressed in God's creation. The Old Testament demonstrates the character of God through the *historical record* and Paul calling upon the natural revelation declared in the Psalm and likens the gospel going out, to God's hands at work obvious in creation, similar in thought to Romans 1:20. Particularly, emphasis in Psalm (19:5) is the sun that universally arrays itself upon the earth after coming out and heating all the earth. The metaphor is one of a gradual start then a "strong man to run his course", here, he uses the LXX exactly.

GNT:
Εις πάσαν την γην εξήλθεν ο φθόγγος αυτών; και εις τα πέρατα της οικουμένης τα ρήματα αυτών.
LXX:
Εις *Into* πάσαν *all* την *the* γην *earth* εξήλθεν *went out* ο φθόγγος αυτών *their sound;* και *and* εις *into* τα *the* πέρατα *boundaries* της *of the* οικουμένης *inhabitable world* τα ρήματα αυτών *their words.*

Henry Alford, qualifies the understanding:

As to the assertion of the preaching of the gospel having gone out into all the world, when as yet a small part of it only had been evangelized, —we must remember that it is not the extent, so much as the universality in character, of this preaching, which the Apostle is here asserting ; that word of God, hitherto confined within the limits of Judea, had now broken those bounds, and was preached in all parts of the earth. See Col. i. 6, 23. 19.[107]

---

107 Henry Alford, Alford's Greek New Testament, Vol., II, Baker Book House, Grand Rapids, Michigan, reprinted 1980, page 422.

NEVERTHELESS THE GOSPEL PROCLAMATION IS HEARD BY
THE CALLING OF THE GENTILES
10:19   DEUTERONOMY 32:21
10:20   ISAIAH 65:1

Paul is stating (vs.10:19,20) the fact of previously made *prophecies* and now *fulfillment* from Moses in Deuteronomy 32:21 and Isaiah 65:1, reference the warnings in those prophecies.

The setting for the citation from Deuteronomy 32:21 is the Song of Moses' the occasion is after the crossing of the Red Sea and the destruction of Pharaoh. Warnings are issued to Israel. Idolatry will bring God's wrath.

The LXX translates the means of provoking God's jealousy by a no-God and the analogy to provoke Israel to jealousy by a no-people. Idolatry is like not having God, a no-God. The no-people is like not having a civilization and community the opposite of what Israel's Theocracy should be. They are the heathen, pagan world. Paul reminds the Gentile Christians of their past state (Romans 11:30; Ephesians 2:11-12).

As Deuteronomy 32:21a with 21c has it: (a)Επ´ over ου [that which is] not θεώ God is analogous to επ´ over (c)ουκ [that which is] not έθνει a people.

S. R. Driver says of what Israel is directed to understand:

They will be rewarded according to the law of righteous retribution: jealousy and vexation (4:24-25) on one side will be requited with jealousy and vexation the other; the "no-God" will be put to shame by a "no-people"; and Israel senseless itself (v.6) will be taught a bitter lesson by a people "senseless" likewise.___ A no-God] a contemptuous designation of the unreal Gods, whom the Israelites followed after (cf. v.17)___ Vanities] הָבֶל (lit. a breadth Is. 57:13) denotes fig. what is evanescent, unsubstantial, worthless: hence of false gods, esp. in Jer:[108]

Disobedience and obstinance are results of ignoring
10:21　　　　　　Isaiah 65:2

In contrast to the Gentiles being brought into the community of the Lord, Paul cites Isaiah 65:2 in this continued recall (v.21) of Isaiah's *prophecy*. The natural results of disobedience and ignoring the gospel are based on the character of God and His relation to His message, in willfully disbelieving and contradicting attitude. This will be the predicted results from this *prophecy and history*.

---

[108] S. R. Driver, A Critical and Exegetical Commentary on Deuteronomy, Charles Scribner and Sons, 1902, page 365.

CHAPTER 9
RESTORATION OF ISRAEL

PRESENT ELECTION IS LIKE THE DAYS OF ELIJAH
MEANS THAT A REMNANT OF JEWS OF ISRAEL ARE SAVED PRESENTLY
11:3   1 KINGS 19:10
11:4   1 KINGS 19:18

THE CHOSEN OF ISRAEL OBTAIN RIGHTEOUSNESS
THE REST ARE HARDENED
11:8   ISAIAH 29:10; DEUTERONOMY 29:4
11:9   PSALM 69:22
11:10   PSALM 69:23

THE FUTURE RESTORATION FAITH IS A MYSTERY
11:26   ISAIAH 59:20-21
11:27   ISAIAH 27:9

DOXOLOGY
11:34   ISAIAH 40:13
11:35   JOB 35:7; 41:11

Paul begins this chapter by asserting that all of Israel is not cast away or rejected by God (μὴ γένοιτο- may it never be!). God's purpose in election preserves a remnant, that is not saved by what the Jews thought would save them, meretricious works, lineal corporeal descent and circumcision. He has already explained how there are 2 Israels. Salvation is determined by grace and applied to the children of promise.

PRESENT ELECTION IS LIKE THE DAYS OF ELIJAH
MEANS THAT A REMNANT OF JEWS OF ISRAEL ARE SAVED PRESENTLY
11:3   1 KINGS 19:10
11:4   1 KINGS 19:18

He couples his introductory formula in a question this time, 11:2, ἢ οὐκ οἴδατε ἐν Ἠλίᾳ τί λέγει ἡ γραφή. Literally, 'Or not know you what the *Scripture says* in Elijah?' He cites Israel's history from 1 Kings. He refers to the time when King Ahab reigned and his wife Jezebel who was a significant in diminishing the worship of Israel's true God.

S. K. Mosiman contributing in ISBE writes this regarding Jezebel:

She was the patron of the prophets of Baal and of the devotees of Asherab (1 Ki 18:19, 20; 19:1, 2) At her instigation the altars of Yahweh were torn down. She inaugurated the first great religious persecution of the church, killing off the prophets of Yahweh with the sword. In all this she aimed at more than a syncretism of the two religions; she planned to destroy the religion of Yahweh root and branch and put that of Baal in its place. In this Ahab did not oppose her, but is guilty of conniving at the policy of his unprincipled wife, if not of heartily concurring in it.[109]

In verse 3 and 4, Paul draws upon the *history* of the Jewish nation to demonstrate his teaching. Chapter 19 of 1 Kings, recounting an event in 9th century B. C., Elijah killing the prophets of Baal and his later transcendence into heaven like Enoch, makes Elijah renown among the Old Testament prophets. His appearance, with Moses on the Mount of Transfiguration (Mark 9:4), testifies to this. Couple this with Malachi 4:5-6 is why Paul can draw upon Elijah and Jewish *prophetic history*. The Jews would be very familiar with this prophet and his works. Elijah was known among the people in Jerusalem at the crucifixion, right before Jesus ended his work on the cross (Matthew 27:47-50). Paul also promotes himself as

---

109 S. K. Mosiman, gen. ed., James Orr, International Standard Bible Encyclopedia, Volume I, Wm. B. Eerdmans Publishing Grand Rapids, Michigan, reprinted 1978, page 79.

a reliable witness to his own testimony by presenting his credentials in verse 1. He has asserted the Jewishness of his gospel in chapter 1:6; 2:9-10, 17, 28-29; 3:1,29; 9:24; 10:12. They are quite familiar with the history. The recall of Jewish history and their propensity into idolatry further presses their need to understand the faithfulness of God's plan for Israel.

The citation recalls the despair in Elijah's response to the Lord and that he is the only one left and they are seeking his life. The divine response of verse 4 is the parallel between then, Elijah not seeing any belief among the nation and now, the apparent unbelief of the nation of the Jews as Paul writes (Romans 10:21). God's plan counters that thinking. He has preserved a remnant. Who is the remnant (λεῖμμα used one time here, 11:5 in NT) Paul speaks of? Paul's mission methodology included to the Jew first as he writes in Romans 1:16, 2:9, and 2:10. Acts chapter 13, 14, 17, 18, 19 and 22, recount his experiences in synagogue attendance. The remnant is not Israel but only part of Israel, as Acts 7:7 and 21:20 indicate. Just as today there are believing Jews. They are part of God's elect (Romans 8:33). In verse 6, he reiterates the common theme in all his letters that it is by grace and not works (Ephesians 2:8-9). He makes a clear separation of grace and works in his statements in verse Romans 11:6, there is no combination method for both to work in God's plan of election.

Let it be clear, the deteriorated Jewish system of works, that is a misapprehension of the Law failed to obtain what they desired (cf. Galatians 2:21).The misapprehension involves a self made religion that requires a merit based system to be justified before God. The true believer understands that system fails because of sin. Paul is not to be misunderstood. He is not diminishing what the Israelites were given, which he reiterates in Romans 9:3-5, otherwise, the actions of Mary and Joseph (cf. Luke 2:21-36) as obedient Israelites would be specious. In that passage, the true Israelites, the believers in the One greater than the Law itself. Simeon and Anna the daughter of Phanuel would have been practicing a vain religion and would not have found the comfort (Luke 2:25) and the redemption of Israel (Luke 2:38).

There is no substitution for God's salvation with a system of self imposed works supposing salvation results. The difference lies in the (ἀρραβὼν – arrhaboôn – pledge money which in purchases is given as a pledge or down payment that the full amount will subsequently be paid[110]) given to those of faith (2 Corinthians 1:22; 2 Corinthians 5:5; Ephesians 1:14).

Johannes Behm writes:

The Spirit whom God has given them is for Christians the guarantee of their full future possession of salvation...Christ by His death is a pledge that Christians will attain the righteousness at the last judgment'.[111]

Fritz Rienecker on ἀρραβὼν notes that, the use of the genitive of apposition, "the guarantee consisting of the Spirit".[112]

John Eadie writes:

The earnest is less than the future inheritance, a mere fraction of it...The work of God's Spirit is never to be undervalued, yet it is only a

---

110 Joseph Henry Thayer, translated revised and enlarged, Greek English-Lexicon of the New Testament, Harper & Brothers, New York, Cincinnati, Chicago, American Book Company, 1889, page 75.
111 Johannes Behm, ed. Gerhard Kittel, trans. Geoffrey Bromiley, (TDNT) Theological Dictionary of the New Testament Vol. I, Wm. B. Eerdmans Publishing Grand Rapids, Michigan, reprinted 1979 10th printing 1979, page 475.
112 Fritz Rienecker, A Linguistic Key to the Greek New Testament Vol 2., Zondervan Publishing House, 1980, page 108.

small thing in relation to future blessedness....The "earnest," in short, is the "inheritance" in miniature, and it is also a pledge that the inheritance shall be ultimately and fully enjoyed. God will not resile from His promise, the Spirit conferred will perfect the enterprise.[113]

THE CHOSEN OF ISRAEL OBTAIN RIGHTEOUSNESS
THE REST ARE HARDENED
11:8   ISAIAH 29:10; DEUTERONOMY 29:4
11:9-10   PSALM 69:22-23

Using the confirmatory formulas (vs.8-10) καθὼς γέγραπται and Καὶ Δαυὶδ λέγει, demonstrates the result of God's election citing (v.8) Isaiah 29:10, with some intimation to Deuteronomy 29:4, in this citation and Psalm 69:22-23 (vs. 9-10) as *prophetic fulfillment.* History tends to repeat itself. The Jews have a notorious history for their spiritual blindness (viz. 40 years wandering in the wilderness). There is peril in unbelief and that warning should always be included in the gospel proclamation. This extends to the individual as well as the whole. Jesus speaks of the same problem in Matthew 15:17. Isaiah *prophesied* this.

A summary of James Denney and his comments on these verses that speak of the 2 aspects of Jewish salvation history follow:[114]

1. The Jews misunderstood the law and that proved their ruin.
2. This misunderstanding led to an incapacity to understand and receive the gospel.
3. The Jews adhered to self righteousness and the law became a

---

113 John Eadie, The John Eadie Greek Text Commentaries, The Ephesians, Baker Book House, Grand Rapids, Michigan, reprinted 1979, from T & T Clark 1883, edition, page 57.
114 James Denney, ed. W. Robertson Nicoll, The Expositor's Greek Testament, Vol. II, Wm. B. Eerdmans Publishing Grand Rapids, Michigan, reprinted 1979, page 678. καὶ εἰς ἀνταπόδομα αὐτοῖς 'and for retribution to them'

means to salvation.
4. This however, is not the final disposition of the Jews as Paul states in Romans 11:11-24.

The words of the Scripture and the *prophesy* Paul introduces with καθὼς γέγραπται, describing hardening are severe. It is best to stay away from thinking that God permitted this to happen, Isaiah says God gave them over to "spirit of stupor". He combines Isaiah 29:10; Deuteronomy 29:4 in verse 8.

Either God is in control of all things or not. Paul has addressed Pharaoh from the time of the Red Sea events in Israel's history in chapter 9 and how the sovereign will of God is in control. A brief list demonstrates how the Scripture is replete with this knowledge of the Lord of the universe and His dealings with mankind.

Some of the examples of the sovereign will of God are:

1. Favorable attitudes - Proverbs 16:7; Psalm 5:12.
2. Wicked acts - Proverbs 16:4; Psalm 105:25; Acts 2:23, Acts 4:28; Joshua 11:20.
3. Overruling sin for good - Genesis 45:8.
4. Calamity - Amos 3:5-6; Isaiah. 45:7, 54:16.
5. Activity of Satan and Demons - 1 Kings 22:19-23; 2 Corinthians 12:7.
6. The smallest things in life - Matthew 10:29 "Are not two sparrows sold for a cent? And yet not one of them will fall to the ground apart from your Father".

The NBDBG defines this "spirit of stupor" that Paul cites from Isaiah as, "fig. for insensibilty of speech" and adds the same word used in 1 Samuel 26:12 and Genesis 2:21 as a deep, deep sleep usually by supernatural agency.[115]

The κατανύξεως (stupor) and the (MT) equivalent תַּרְדֵּמָה (tardeòmaòh tar-day-maw'), v. 8, are remarked on by William White in the TWOT:

> Deep sleep, sleepiness; lethargy, This feminine noun developed from the verbal root, radam, appears seven times in the OT. The initial occurrence is in Gen 2:21, "a deep sleep." It is used to describe the state in which Abraham had his vision of God (Gen 15:12). In I Sam 26:12, "a deep sleep" is sent upon Saul and his army when pursuing David. The same connotation of "insensitivity" to danger is presented in Isa 29:10 and Job 4:13; 33:15. All of these texts present "sleep" as the profundity of divine intervention. It is God who casts such sleep or sleeplessness upon his chosen servant.[116]

Heinrich Meyer says of Romans 11:8, the "spirit of stupor", that it is a demonic influence:

> 'πνεῦμα κατανύξεως Heb. רוּחַ תַּרְדֵּמָה, i.e. a spirit producing stupefaction, which is obviously a daemonic spirit. Comp. 2 Corinthians 4:4; Ephesians 2:2.[117]

Heinrich Greeven further elaborates the explanation when he writes:

---

115 Francis Brown, S. R. Driver, Charles Briggs, (NBDBG) trans., Edward Robinson, The New Brown Driver Briggs Gesenius Hebrew Aramaic English Lexicon, Associated Publishers and Authors, Inc., Lafayette, Indiana, 1980, page 922.
116 William White, ed., R. Laird Harris, (TWOT) Theological Wordbook of the Old Testament, Vol 2, Moody press, Chicago, 1980, page 834.
117 H. A. W. Meyer's, Critical and Exegetical Commentary on the New Testament, Romans, Vol. V., Alpha Greek Library, Winona Lake Wisconsin, reprinted 1980, page 431.

Paul finds in the words of Is. confirmation for his contention that the hardening of so many Jews is no less God's work than the election of Israel. The context allows us only one rendering of πνεῦμα κατανύξεως, namely, "spirit of stupification." This corresponds to the sense of the reference in Is.[118]

Joseph Henry Thayer defines the 'slumber' as:

It is insensibility or torpor of mind, such as extreme grief easily produces, hence a "spirit of stupor", which renders their souls torpid so insensible that they are not affected at all by the offer made them of salvation through the Messiah.[119]

Paul says these these calamities are the result of the action of God against the Israel and are *fulfilled and fulfilling prophecy*. A continuing lack of sensibility to the gospel maintains. Paul adds to the figurative language these descriptive words to detail the deficient perception: eyes ὀφθαλμοὺς (ophthalmos) with no seeing Βλέπω (blepoô), ears, οὖς (ous) with no hearing ἀκούω (akouoô). This condition has continued from Israel's history until the present day. He states the same in 2 Corinthians 3:15. John 12:39-40 expresses the same idea citing Isaiah 6:10.

He also cites David in Romans 11:9-10, from the Messianic Psalm 69:22-23. adding to his presentation of Israel's condition. In verses 20-21 of that Psalm, the suffering and lament over Christ's suffering is detailed. The imprecation to His enemies follows. The result of enjoying the blessings and place of security and material nourishment by being God's chosen

---

118 Heinrich Greeven, ed. Gerhard Kittel, trans. Geoffrey Bromiley, (TDNT) Theological Dictionary of the New Testament Vol. III, Wm. B. Eerdmans Publishing Grand Rapids, Michigan, reprinted 1979, 10th printing 1979, page 626.
119 Joseph Henry Thayer, translated revised and enlarged, Greek English-Lexicon of the New Testament, Harper & Brothers, New York, Cincinnati, Chicago, American Book Company, 1889, page 334.

people have instead become the opposite for Israel due to their blindness and hardening because of their rejection of the Lord Jesus Christ. Many of the Jews of Jesus' time saw His works of miracles and still did not believe. This place of blessing becomes a place of destruction for them by unbelief as retribution for rejection of the Messiah.

Handley Carr Glyn Moule comments:

> The point of the quotation is that the Psalm indicates a judicial turning of blessings into curses, and a judicial blindness and impotence of the soul, as the way in which retribution would come on Messiah's enemies.[120]

The synonyms, παγίς (pagis) snare and θήρα (theôra) trap, couples with ἀνταπόδομα (antapodoma) recompense, shows how the place of blessing (τράπεζα trapeza, table) yields the opposite.

The TDNTA says of the figure of the table in Romans 11:9:

> In Rom. 11:9 the table is a figure of nourishment. What should contribute to life becomes a snare; the law is probably meant (cf. 11:7; 9:31).[121]

This results in punishment to them. The result is σκάνδαλον (skandalon), stumbling block.

The TDNTA says of the figure of the stumbling:

---

120 H. C. G. Moule, Studies in Romans, Kregel Publications, Grand Rapids, Michigan, reprinted 1982, page 190.
121 (TDNTA) Theological Dictionary of the New Testament, ed., Gerhard Kittel and Gerhard Friedrich trans., Geoffrey W. Bromiley, Abridged in One Volume, page 1077. 1985, [L. GOPPELT, VIII, 209-15]

In the NT, as in the OT, the issue in skándalon is one's relation to God. The skándalon is an obstacle to faith and hence a cause of falling and destruction.[122]

C. E. B. Cranfield remarks on the imagery of the table:

And David says: 'Let their table become a snare and a trap and a stumbling-block and a retribution to them; let their eyes be darkened so that they cannot see, and do thou bow down their back continually.' The latter of the two Old Testament quotations in these verses is Ps. 69.22-23. This psalm is one which was much used in the early Church as a testimony of the ministry, and especially the passion, of Christ. Paul here applies to the unbelieving majority of Israel words which were originally the psalmist's imprecation on his persecutors but which, when the psalm is understood messianically, are naturally referred to the opponents of Christ. The general sense of the first sentence is no doubt a wish that even the good things which these enemies enjoy may prove to be a cause of disaster to them. The original imagery has been variously explained: for example, with reference to the skin or cloth, spread out on the ground by nomads, upon which the feast was laid, which could entangle the feet of the feasters, if they sprang up suddenly at the approach of danger, or with reference to poisoned viands intended for particular individuals which those who have prepared them are themselves forced to eat.[123]

Romans 11:10 "LET THEIR EYES BE DARKENED TO SEE NOT, AND BEND THEIR BACKS FOREVER."

In verse 10 he uses, συγκάμπτω, according to Joseph Henry Thayer:

---

122 Ibid., page 937. [G. STÄHLIN, VII, 339-58]
123 Cranfield, Romans, A Shorter Commentary, Wm. B. Eerdmans Publishing Grand Rapids, Michigan, copyright T & T Clark, 1985, page 234.

metaphorically to subject one to error and hardness of heart, a figure taken from bowing the back by captives compelled to pass under the yoke.[124]

They are enslaved to blindness spiritually. Until such a time of regeneration this punishment continues. The Jews, Israel are no longer God's chosen people, they are an apostate national entity. Matthew 23:38-39 says "Behold, your house is being left to you desolate! 'For I say to you, from now on you will not see Me until you say, BLESSED IS HE WHO COMES IN THE NAME OF THE LORD!'"

W. Sanday, A. C. Headlam remark on the continued spiritual blindness "down to this very day" that Paul references:

ἕως τῆς σήμερον ἡμέρας. cf. Acts vii. 51... St. Stephen's speech illustrates more in detail the logical assumptions which underlie St. Paul's quotations. The chosen people have from the beginning shown the same obstinate adherence to their own views and a power of resisting the Holy Ghost ; and God has throughout punished them for their obstinacy by giving them over to spiritual blindness.[125]

THE FUTURE RESTORATION FAITH IS A MYSTERY
11:26   ISAIAH 59:20-21
11:27   ISAIAH 27:9

The Gentiles are beneficiaries of this *prophecy*. Romans 11:25 declares the mystery of the partial hardening and future deliverance of Israel. What is critical to understand is what

---

124 Joseph Henry Thayer, translated revised and enlarged, Greek English-Lexicon of the New Testament, Harper & Brothers, New York, Cincinnati, Chicago, American Book Company, 1889, page 592.
125 W. Sanday, A. C. Headlam, The International Critical Commentary, Critical and Exegetical Commentary on the Epistle to the Romans Edinburgh: T & T Clark, 1902, page 315.

Paul means by, and so all Israel will be saved; in verse 25 and 26, before he cites Isaiah 59:20-21 and Isaiah 27:9.

Paul has informed the reader that some of the Jews believed, like in the days of Elijah (Romans 11:5), there is always a remnant of the faithful in the history of Israel according to history and prophecy. Despite Israel reaching a nadir in their history at the first coming of Christ, a remnant was always present (cf. Luke 2:25, 2:34; Romans 9:27).

So a remnant is saved and the rest hardened, temporarily, yet God's "gifts and calling" are irrevocable. Eschatologically speaking, the Jews in majority numbers, collectively will be saved upon their recognition of the Messiah.

A parallel of the "fullness of the Gentiles" and "and so all Israel will be saved" should be seen here. Inasmuch, as the gospel is preached universally, i.e. to all and at this time some of the Gentiles, mainly people from every race and nation, but some Jews come and enter the Faith and the Church, so also, a time is coming when mainly Jews will enter the Faith and the Church. It is a future event. Not every individual from the Gentiles is saved, nor will every individual from the Jews will be saved. From the perspective of the Scriptures these are the 2 categories of people. Whether one has claim to the ethnic origin Jew or not, God knows what He is talking about and the identity of the Jews for these *prophetic* words, based on Scriptural authority.

CHAPTER 11	JEWS ACTION/RESULT	GENTILES RESULT/ACTION
v11	TRANSGRESSION	SALVATION
v11	JEALOUSY	SALVATION
v12	TRANSGRESSION	RICHES FOR WORLD
v12	FAILURE	RICHES FOR GENTILES
v12	JEWISH FULFILLMENT	MUCH MORE

v15	REJECTION	RECONCILIATION FOR WORLD
v15	ACCEPTANCE	LIFE FROM THE DEAD
v25	PARTIAL HARDENING	FULLNESS OF GENTILES
v25-26	ALL ISRAEL WILL BE SAVED	FULLNESS OF GENTILES HAS COME IN

THE FUTURE RESTORATION FAITH IS A MYSTERY
11:26   ISAIAH 59:20-21
11:27   ISAIAH 27:9

In reference to the Redeemer-Deliverer (גָּאַל gaòal *gaw-al'*, NT equivalent, ῥύομαι rhuomai) of Isaiah 59:20. This is the future *prophetic* guarantee for all Israel. Cited by Paul here remarked by R. Laird Harris in the TWOT:

> Finally, there is the very common usage prominent in the Psalms and prophets that God is Israel's Redeemer who will stand up for his people and vindicate them. There may be a hint of the Father's near kinship or ownership in the use of this word. A redemption price is not usually cited, though the idea of judgment on Israel's oppressors as a ransom is included in Isa 43:1-3. God, as it were, redeems his sons from a bondage worse than slavery.[126]

Paul goes on to say, using the analogy of the olive tree and the grafting in of the branches from the wild olive tree (Gentiles) and asserting that the natural branches (Jews) will be grafted in again to the cultivated olive tree. The basis for the grafting in is faith.

This is also a mystery (μυστήριον musteôrion). Not the mysteries inferred from the pagan, cultic, philosophical or Gnostic world around Rome, where rites, esoteric knowledge,

---

[126] White, William ed., R. Laird Harris, (TWOT) Theological Wordbook of the Old Testament, Vol 2, Moody Press, Chicago, 1980, page 144.

special initiations and celebrations bring the participant some state of perceived salvation (Colossians 2:18).

Here, mystery means (Romans 11:25), according to Joseph Henry Thayer:

a hidden purpose or counsel; secret will ... used of certain single events decreed by God having reference to His Kingdom of the salvation of men, Ro. xi 25; 1 Cor. xv. 51.[127]

The question is what Paul means by 'mystery' and the connection to ἵνα μὴ ἦτε ἑαυτοῖς φρόνιμοι, (in order that not you in yourselves be wise)?

Henry Alford endeavors this explanation on mystery (Romans 11:25):

For (I do not rest this on mere hope or probability, but have direct revelation of the Holy Spirit as to its certainty) I would not have you ignorant, brethren (see reff.,—used by the Apostle to announce, either as here some authoritative declaration of divine truth, or some facts in his own history not previously known to his readers), of this mystery (of this mystery μυστ. Tholuck in his 4th edition classifies the meanings thus : (1) *such matters of fact, as are inaccessible to reason, and can only be known through revelation* : (2) *such matters as are patent facts, but the process of which cannot be entirely taken in by the reason.* He adds a third sense,—that, which is no mystery *in itself,* but *by its figurative import.*[128]

---

127 Joseph Henry Thayer, translated revised and enlarged, Greek English-Lexicon of the New Testament, Harper & Brothers, New York, Cincinnati, Chicago, American Book Company, 1889, page 420.
128 Henry Alford, Alford's Greek New Testament, Vol., II Baker Book House, Grand Rapids, Michigan, reprinted 1980, page 434. He adds that Tholuck gives these references for the reasons: (1) Romans 16:25; 1 Corinthians 2:7-10; Ephesians 1:9, 3:4, 6:19; Colossians 1:26 (2) 1 Corinthians 14:2,13:2; Ephesians 5:32; 1 Timothy 3:9, 16 (3) Matthew 13:11; Revelation 1:20, 17:5; 2 Thessalonians 2:7.

His conclusion is: The first meaning is evidently that in our text:—'a prophetic event, unattainable by human knowledge, but revealed from the secrets of God')[129]

There is support for this view since Christian converts believe what is contrary to what the world believes concerning God's plan of redemption (John 17:3). It is necessary for believers to know of this mystery since Paul says it is (1 Corinthians 2:7). Paul is well aware that this mystery is written down and taught (1 Corinthians 2:12-13; 1 Thessalonians 2:13). The Bible itself (Romans 16:25-26) is a mystery and the revealed word of God is linked in what Paul has written here. Paul's admonition "in order that not you may be wise from yourselves", is most appropriate at all times among God's people. It is also by Paul's writing a letter to the Roman church that this mystery is revelatory (1 Corinthians 7:10, 12, 25, 40; Luke 1:3).

Charles Hodges sees μυστήριον, mystery this way and writes:

It is therefore used in reference to all the doctrines of the gospel which are not the truths of reason, but matters of divine revelation; Romans16:25; 1 Corinthians 2:7; 4:1; Ephesians 6:19, etc. Hence ministers are called stewards of the mysteries (*i.e.,* of the revelations) of God. It is also used of some one doctrine, considered as previously unknown and undiscoverable by human reason, however simple and intelligible in its own nature. Thus, the fact that the Gentiles should be admitted into the church of God, Paul calls a *mystery,* Ephesians 1:9; 3:4. Any future event, therefore, which could be known only by divine revelation, is a mystery. The fact that all should not die, though all should be changed, was a mystery, 1 Corinthians 15:51. In like manner, here, when Paul says, "I would not, brethren, have you ignorant of this mystery," he means to say, that the event to which he referred, was one which, depending on no secondary cause, but on the divine purpose,

---

129 Ibid.

could be known only by divine revelation. This description is certainly far more suitable to the annunciation of a prophecy, than to the statement of a fact which might have been confidently inferred from what God had already revealed.[130]

Robert Haldane, on mystery in Romans 11:25, captures the admonition that Paul is communicating to the church:

This mystery was opened to prevent the Gentiles from being *wise in their own conceits,* that is, from being puffed up on account of the preference they now enjoyed. Ignorance of the Scriptures is the cause of high-mindedness in Christians. They are often arrogant and contemptuous through want of knowledge. In the absence of real knowledge, they often suppose they have a true understanding of things with which they are still unacquainted, and are thus vain and conceited.[131]

The mystery relates to belief, faith, Jude 1:3 ... for the faith which was once for all handed down to the saints.

DOXOLOGY
11:34   ISAIAH 40:13
11:35   JOB 35:7; 41:11

The final citation in Romans 11:34-35 are Isaiah 40:13 and Job 35:7; 41:11 respectively. In his doxology that completes the idea this the mystery the church embraces for all time is beyond our measuring capacity and is inscrutable. The Scriptures are not sourced from human reason. What we know about God and His purposes are very limited, however, the knowledge we do have is sufficient for salvation. These

---

130 Charles Hodge, Commentary on the Epistle to the Romans, Philadelphia: Alfred Martien, 1214 Chestnut Street, 1873, page 586.
131 Robert Haldane, Exposition of the Epistle to the Romans; with remarks on the Commentaries of Dr. Macknight, Professor Moses Stuart, and Professor Tholuck, New York, Robert Carter, 58 Canal Street, and Pittsburgh, 56 Market Street. 1847, page 553.

citations also form a unique category of Old Testament citations, citing Old Testament *historical record* to demonstrate the character of God and corroborate Paul's assertions. The usual confirmatory formula, for fulfilled prophecy introduction "just as it has been written" is not present.

He begins with Ὦ βάθος *deep*, ('O the deep things' of God, things hidden and above man's scrutiny, especially the Divine counsels, 1 Corinthians 2:10).[132] God's sovereign design for all time given as redemption for mankind is so full of abundance for our good and so deep that one cannot get to the end of the path to find a human finite explanation. He is beyond mankind to comprehend, but what He has revealed is adequate and sufficient for faith.

Archibald Robertson remarks:

Paul's argument concerning God's elective grace and goodness has carried him to the heights and now he pauses on the edge of the precipice as he contemplates God's wisdom and knowledge, fully conscious of his inability to sound the bottom with the plummet of human reason and words.[133]

---

132 Joseph Henry Thayer, translated revised and enlarged, Greek English-Lexicon of the New Testament, Harper & Brothers, New York, Cincinnati, Chicago, American Book Company, 1889, page 92.
133 A. T. Robertson, Word Pictures in the New Testament, Vol. IV, The Epistles of Paul, Baker Book House, Grand Rapids, MI, 1931, page 400.

Chapter 10
Righteousness of God in Believer's Lives

Law of Christ and Christian practice in persecution
12:19   Proverbs 20:22
12:20   Proverbs 25:21-22

Duty to one's neighbor
13:9   Exodus 20:13ff.; Leviticus 19:18

Duties to weak and strong Christians be liberal
14:11   Isaiah 45:23

Reason we should please others
15:3   Psalm 69:9

Consequences of the work of Christ accept others
15:9   Psalm 18:49 or 2 Samuel 22:50
15:10   Deuteronomy 32:43
15:11   Psalm 117:1
15:12   Isaiah 11:10

Paul's new plans create new works
15:21   Isaiah 52:15

In Paul's letter to the Church at Rome, it must be noted the commonly accepted date of the Neronian persecution is 64 A.D. The Epistle had been written a few years earlier, probably around 57 A.D. Christians of Rome had to endure the coming persecution being blamed for the great conflagration.

Philip Schaff writes of the severe physical pain the Christians endured in his history of the Christian Church:

Under this wanton charge of incendiarism, backed by the equally groundless charge of misanthropy and unnatural vice, there began a carnival of blood such as even heathen Rome never saw before or since. [524] It was the answer of the powers of hell to the mighty preaching of the two chief apostles, which had shaken heathenism to its centre. A "vast multitude" of Christians was put to death in the most shocking manner. Some were crucified, probably in mockery of the punishment of Christ, [525] some sewed up in the skins of wild beasts and exposed to the voracity of mad dogs in the arena. The satanic tragedy reached its climax at night in the imperial gardens on the slope of the Vatican (which embraced, it is supposed, the present site of the place and church of St. Peter): Christian men and women, covered with pitch or oil or resin, and nailed to posts of pine, were lighted and burned as torches for the amusement of the mob; while Nero, in fantastical dress, figured in a horse race, and displayed his art as charioteer. Burning alive was the ordinary punishment of incendiaries; but only the cruel ingenuity of this imperial monster, under the inspiration of the devil, could invent such a horrible system of illumination.[134]

---

134 Philip Schaff, History of the Christian Church, Charles Scribner's Sons, New York, Vol I, 1889, pp. 381-382.[524] We do not know the precise date of the massacre. Mosheim fixes it on November, Renan on August, a.d. 64. Several weeks or months at all events must have passed after the fire. If the traditional date of Peter's crucifixion be correct there would be an interval of nearly a year between the conflagration, July 19, 64, and his martyrdom, June 29th.[525] "Crucibus affixi," says Tacitus. This would well apply to Peter, to whom our Lord had prophesied such a death, John 21:18,19. Tertullian says: "Romae Petrus passioni Dominicae adaequatur" (De Praescript. Haeret., c. 36; comp. Adv. Marc., IV. 5; Scorpiace, 15). According to a later tradition he was, at his own request, crucified with his head downwards, deeming himself unworthy to be crucified as was his Lord. This is first mentioned in the Acta Pauli, c. 81, by Origen (in Euseb. H. E., III. 1) and more clearly by Jerome (Catal. 1); but is doubtful, although such cruelties were occasionally practised (see Josephus, Bell. Jud.,V. 11, 1). Tradition mentions also the martyrdom of Peter's wife, who was cheered by the apostle on her way to the place of execution and exhorted to remember the Lord on the cross (μέμνησο τοῦ Κυρίου). Clement of Alexandria, Strom. VII. 11, quoted by Eusebius, H. E., III. 30. The orderly execution of Paul by the sword indicates a regular legal process before, or more probably at least a year after, the Neronian persecution in which his Roman citizenship would scarcely have been respected. See page 326.

The world that Christianity entered was the severest anti-God environment that may ever have existed. Previously in chapter 6 some of the environmental hazards for Christians then and now were addressed. This is the context of his letter to Rome.

LAW OF CHRIST AND CHRISTIAN PRACTICE IN PERSECUTION
12:19   PROVERBS 20:22
12:20   PROVERBS 25:21-22

Paul's method is doctrine first then practice. In Romans chapter 12 he does just this. The citations he uses are: 12:19-20 from Proverbs 20:22 and in 12:20 from Proverbs 25:21ff. In verse 2, he starts by telling us what is the revealed will of God for the believer. As unnatural as it is, not taking vengeance is God's will. When contemplating the ills, sufferings, humiliations, pain, torture, mocking, family rejection, deprivation and degradation that believer's might experience in this world and the desire to strike back at those who perpetrate these things on account of one's faith in Christ, Paul says, "Never pay back evil for evil to anyone". Christians will have enemies that will inflict harm of various magnitudes. It is happening in the world today. A brief research project of contemporary news will always reveal worldwide persecution of Christians. The natural reaction is to destroy one's enemies. Justice is always sought by even depraved men. That is why films and stories that portray justice themes are always popular. The Book of Esther portrays justice (cf. The Feast of Purim), but it is the Lord that performs it through whatever means He chooses, even though God's name is not mentioned in Esther (Song of Solomon is the other). He delivered the Jews from death at the hands of Haman (Esther 3:6), to which justice is delivered (Esther 9:25). If vengeance and retribution were left up to us, it would never make the mark. It may be too little or too much. Man cannot appropriately deliver it. Only an ethically pure individual can give justice. There is only one of those (Romans 3:4). It is His proper domain.

Louis Berkhof points out regarding the wrath of God and retributive justice:

Retributive justice, which relates to the infliction of penalties. It is an expression of the divine wrath. While in a sinless world there would be no place for its exercise, it necessarily holds a very prominent place in a world full of sin. On the whole the Bible stresses the reward of the righteous more than the punishment of the wicked; but even the latter is sufficiently prominent. Rom. 1:32; 2:9; 12:19; II Thess. 1:8, and many other passages. It should be noted that, while man does not merit the reward which he receives, he does merit the punishment which is meted out to him.[135]

Paul using the confirmatory formula, γέγραπται γάρ, "for it has been written", indicates that God's vengeance is *prophetic*. For the Christians in the Church at Rome, retribution will be carried out perfectly in the future, it is not the place of the believer to have. It is also indicative of the *third use of the Law,* it is an axiom to live by as a guide.

The reason we should not take revenge is because of God's will. This is an individual rule for the believer in persecution. It does not apply to governments which operate under different rules (Romans 13:4). Also, this is not teaching the negation of self defense in ordinary civil experience or injustice (Acts 16:37-38, chs. 22, 24). With Paul, he addresses wrongful harm (cf. Acts 9:25 with 2 Corinthians 11:33) and appealing to civil government as a citizen (Acts 25:11, 28:19). The Mosaic code (Exodus 22:2-3) speaks of appropriate force used in one's own home. Also, not excluded, are lawsuits when harmed. Remember any general lawsuit prohibition that some Christians think is prohibited universally would be a misapprehension of 1

---

135 Louis Berkhof, Systematic Theology, Wm. B. Eerdmans Publishing Grand Rapids, Michigan, reprinted 1977, page 75.

Corinthians 6:1-7. In that particular case, Paul is speaking about Christians suing civilly outside the church rather than settling matters among themselves internally.

Regarding persecution, Jesus is the originator and model for this action. The reading of Isaiah 53 tells of the deportment of Jesus. It was necessary for Him to do these things and remain silent without exacting revenge, and He could have (Matthew 26:51). By not taking revenge and retaliation, God's purpose is fulfilled. Kindness being returned for evil is the intent. Showing kindness to a Christian's enemies might bring their enemy to a place of contrition and repentance and is in line with the action of God in redemption (cf. Romans 2:4). In the cross, God was reconciling the world to Himself (Romans 5:10).

James Denney points out the meaning of the "coals":

Proverbs 25:21 f. exactly as in LXX. The meaning of "heaping burning coals on his head" is hardly open to doubt. It must refer to the burning pain of shame and remorse which the man feels whose hostility is repaid by love. This is the only kind of vengeance the Christian is at liberty to contemplate.[136]

However, the acts of evil men might be returned to them by conversion (Acts 17:30) or further judgment in the end (Acts 17:31). It is His intent that all believe and come to the knowledge of the truth (1 Timothy 2:4). Nevertheless, the context has to do with leaving room for the wrath of God, a real possibility if salvation and mercy are not received by the enemy inflicting harm upon God's people. Wrath remains a real possibility. If the result of the believer's action is the remorse,

---

[136] James Denney, ed., W. Robertson Nicoll, The Expositor's Greek Testament, Vol. II, Wm. B. Eerdmans Publishing Grand Rapids, Michigan, reprinted 1979, page 694.

repentance and contrition of their enemy then God's mercy triumphs. But, if the enemy does not, then the result will be handled in the final judgment, in God's hands.

There is a limit to God's patience and time will run out. Revelation 20:15 says, "And if anyone's name was not found written in the book of life, he was thrown into the lake of fire."

The principle of Lex Talionis is actually a restrictive precept that applies an equitable retaliation for harm from one to another. It controls the wild inclination for retaliation, like desiring to take 2 eyes for the 1 eye. Civil government has developed the concept of monetary compensation for tort with a system of judges and civil courts (Exodus 21). The Mosaic code (Deuteronomy 19) also provided for "cities of refuge" so that the motive for hot revenge in cases of accidental murder could be curtailed. Furthermore, litigiousness is not to be the norm in other matters for the believer.

DUTY TO ONE'S NEIGHBOR
13:9   EXODUS 20:13FF.; LEVITICUS 19:18

After addressing the duties of the state and the duties that Christians have to a legitimate government (Romans 13:1-7), Paul now switches the topic to duties one has to his neighbor. Just as Christians have an obligation to legitimate government because authority comes from God, so do Christians have an obligation to their neighbor. He now cites in 13:9, Exodus 20:13ff.; Leviticus 19:18. Paul is pointing out that obligation to their neighbor. This is the *third use of the Law*. It is a continuing debt or obligation that is Jesus' definition of the second greatest commandment Matthew 22:39 "The second is like it, 'YOU SHALL LOVE YOUR NEIGHBOR AS YOURSELF.'" Paul is in line with what Jesus taught in this matter also in the Lord's prayer. Matthew 6:12 uses (debt, ὀφείλημα) the same root word as here, as in the Lord's prayer to forgive sin. The word debt, here, means literally to owe money, but used metaphorically here to be under obligation for what is owed.

Christian subjection and obligation to government varies from season to season and jurisdictional region and with changing legislation and regulation. Government is legitimate if it is subject to the parameters that Paul has put forth. The 2 basic principles of legitimate government are protecting the innocent law abiding citizens and punishing evil doers who harm those citizens bringing violence, disorder, crimes against persons, property and morality that harm society and civil authority, generally destroying law and order. (Romans 13:3-5).

Government has the right to apply punishment (cf. the 2 thieves being crucified with Jesus, Matthew 27:38). Christians should always be going about their lawful business. However, sometimes governments do run amuck when they violate the parameters of God ordained operation. History is replete with examples that always exist. Christians in these circumstances might risk death for non-compliance (cf. Daniel 3:6, 11; Acts 5:27-33). There is no prohibition of self defense in the New Testament in ordinary civil matters.

Government compliance can be very transient. This is not true regarding the admonition to love your neighbor, that is perpetual.

Heinrich Meyer remarks on the Paul's shift from obligation to civil government to one's neighbor in verse 8:

Μηδενὶ μηδὲν ὀφείλετε] negatively the same thing, only generally referred to the relation to everybody—and therewith Paul returns to the general duty of Christians—which was before said positively in Romans 13:7 : ἀπόδοτε πᾶσι τὰς ὀφειλάς. By this very parallel, and decisively by the subjective negations, ὀφείλετε is determined to be imperative: "Leave toward no one any obligation unfulfilled, reciprocal love excepted," wherein you neither can, nor moreover are expected, ever fully to discharge your obligation. The inexhaustibility of the duty of love, the claims of which are not discharged, but renewed and accumulated with fulfilment, is expressed.[137]

He cites the second table of the Law and responsibility morally to one's neighbor (Romans 13:9).

DUTIES TO WEAK AND STRONG CHRISTIANS BE LIBERAL
14:11   ISAIAH 45:23

Paul shifts the topic to scruples and principles of conscience. These exist in the Christian community. The nature of one's faith s categorized as weak or strong. Those with many scruples regarding food, days or the drinking of wine are weak. Those that are weak have doubts regarding the legitimacy of their actions in regard to these matters. This disposition restricts and inhibits their action. Their prejudices dominate, particularly eating meat and drinking wine and strong drink. He brings this same topic up in 1 Corinthians 8 and Colossians 2.

This is a summary from Frederic Godet advancing several points as to the identity who these weak Christians, addressed by Paul, might be associated with.[138]

1. Christian party advocating abstinence from eating flesh and drinking wine and considering some days holier than other days.
2. Ebionites and Essenes origin bring an ascetic dualism practice of abstinence into their Christian practice.

---

137 H. A. W. Meyer's, Critical and Exegetical Commentary on the New Testament, Romans, Vol. V., Alpha Greek Library, Winona Lake Wisconsin, reprinted 1980, page 494. Greek quotes in order {To no one nothing owe}; {render to all their dues}; {owe}
138 Frederic Godet, St Paul's Epistle to the Roman Theological Library. trans. A Cusin, new series., Vol. II, Edinburgh: T & T Clark, 38 George Street. 1881, page 326-329.

3. Christians with Jewish origins unwilling to eat meat and drink wine offered to idols. However, the Law did not prohibit the eating of flesh of animals and drinking wine, but of certain unclean meat.
4. Christians adhering to Antediluvian precepts like Genesis 1:29. Not until Genesis 9:3 that meat eating was expressly permitted. By returning to "a primitive regimen"[139] they believed there would not be any compromise of Christian principle.

All these possible differences show up in the church, so Paul wants to address mutual toleration and the maintenance of harmony[140] as the solution.

In Romans 14:11, Paul cites Isaiah 45:23, the ultimate solution for the diverse ideas in the church regarding differences is a matter of *prophecy*. Judging one another ends with the understanding that Christ is the universal final authority of all.

Heinrich Meyer states:

Thus the proposition of Romans 14:10, πάντες γὰρ κ.τ.λ.—although in and by itself it required no scriptural proof—receives, nevertheless, a hallowed confirmation, which makes the injustice of the previously censured judging and despising the more apparent, because it encroaches on the universal final judgment of God. The citation is Isaiah 45:23, quoted very freely with deviations, partly of memory, partly intentional, from the LXX., and abbreviated. In Isaiah, God certifies upon His oath that all men (including the Gentiles) shall render to Him adoring homage. This divine utterance Messianic, because promising the universal triumph of the theocracy—is here taken by Paul in the light of that highest final historical fulfilment

---

139 Ibid., page 328.
140 Ibid., page 329.

which will take place at the judgment of the world.[141]

Additionally, the matters of scruples in the Christian church has to do with knowledge. If, for instance new converts enter the church and have scruples regarding eating of certain foods, then it would be inappropriate at first circumstance, to have a church dinner, lunch or breakfast with these scrupulously designated foods on the menu. If however, once knowledge increases, then it would be inappropriate to adopt and force these scruples as the new standard for church food events. The weak scrupulous Christians that might still be adhering to these scruples, after being taught should then remain silent and tolerate the other believers.

This topic can get out of control quickly. There have been prominent contemporary television preachers that have advocated certain diets derived from the Old Testament clean and unclean animal lists and applying them to Christians today.

Currently, some Christian sects promote certain diets. There is also an abundance of books for sale promoting Christian diets. This is a large topic. Diets and foods have been advocated for adherence throughout church history by various groups. The Council of Jerusalem in Acts 15, indicates the magnitude of the concern, in that, it handled some of the food conflicts that came up in the early church.

For the believers, this gets into a dangerous area. Instead of making progress in matters of faith, they promoted a regressive approach, creating additional scruples. Jesus declared all food "clean" (cf. Mark 7:19 and Acts 10:10-15). There are no dietary

---

141 H. A. W. Meyer's, Critical and Exegetical Commentary on the New Testament, Romans, Vol. V., Alpha Greek Library, Winona Lake Wisconsin, reprinted 1980, page 514.

proscriptions or endorsements in the New Testament. Paul writes in Romans 14:17-18, "for the kingdom of God is not eating and drinking, but righteousness and peace and joy in the Holy Spirit. For he who in this *way* serves Christ is acceptable to God and approved by men".

Joe M. Sprinkle makes this insightful summary capturing the topic's greater question, essence of clean and unclean:

The abolition of the food laws conveys deep theological significance. The division of animals into clean and unclean symbolized the separation between Israelites and Gentiles. The abolition of the kosher laws then symbolizes a breaking down of the barrier between Jews and Gentiles. As is seen in God's lesson to Peter in Acts 10-11, God now declares the Gentiles "clean." In the new messianic age the principle that God's people are to be separate (holy) from the world remains, but the lines drawn are no longer ethnic in character.[142]

REASON WE SHOULD PLEASE OTHERS
15:3   PSALM 69:9

Romans 15:3 is another *fulfilled prophecy*, citing the Messianic Psalm 69:9 as he has done before. Christ is the model for the believer's deportment in the present age making this *the 3rd use of the Law* also. The strong are to bear the burden and put up with (v.1 βαστάζω, bastazoô) the scruples of the weak. The word is used literally in John 19:17 and figuratively in Luke 14:27.

Charles Hodge writes:

We that are strong, (οἱ δυνατοὶ) *strong* in reference to the subject of discourse, *i.e.* faith, especially faith in the Christian doctrine of the

---

[142] Joe M. Sprinkle, Baker Theological Dictionary of the Bible, ed. Walter A. Elwell, Baker Books, Grand Rapids, Michigan, 1996, page 102.

lawfulness of all kinds of food, and the abrogation of the Mosaic law. *Ought to bear i.e.* ought to tolerate, (βαστάζω).The *infirmities*, τὰ ἀσθενήματα that is, the prejudices, errors, and faults which arise from weakness of faith.[143]

It should be emphasized that throughout this discussion by Paul, he never asserts that the weak should set the standards of the church regarding these matters addressed. There is a difference between weak Christians and Pharisees. The Pharisees rules were false and overbearing, Paul does not mention them here, but in Galatians. Jesus disregarded and spoke against the Pharisees (cf. Mathew 12:1-4; Luke 11:37-38).

Consequences of the work of Christ accept others	
15:9	Psalm 18:49 or 2 Samuel 22:50
15:10	Deuteronomy 32:43
15:11	Psalm 117:1
15:12	Isaiah 11:10

Paul goes on to exhort the readers with these additional groups of Old Testament citations, all in the *prophetic context* coupled *with the Law's 3rd use,* giving the attitude the church should have. These Old Testament citations are mainly and literally from the LXX.

Charles Hodge summarizes:

The effect is considered as accomplished. The apostle's language is, as usual, concise. There are two consequences of the work of Christ which he here presents; the one, that the truth of God has been vindicated by the fulfillment of the promises made to the Jews; and the other, that the Gentiles have been led to praise God for his mercy.[144]

---

143 Charles Hodge, Commentary on the Epistle to the Romans, Philadelphia: Alfred Martien, 1214 Chestnut Street.1873, page 680.
144 Ibid., page 685.

PAUL'S NEW PLANS CREATE NEW WORKS
15:21   ISAIAH 52:15

Paul has already make the demonstration by citing the Old Testament that the gospel has come to the Gentiles. In 15:21 he expresses desire to establish new churches. Besides directly cited here, Paul is the evangelist to the Gentiles (Gal. 1:16; Rom. 15:20; 1 Cor. 15:1; 2 Cor. 10:16; Acts 14:10; 17:18). This is seen as a *prophetic fulfillment* of his ministry to the heathen.

He cites from the LXX Isaiah 52:15b, omitting 'for' ὅτι, in Romans 15:21 ἀλλὰ καθὼς γέγραπται (but as it is has been written), the LXX has Isaiah 52:15b begins with ὅτι οις (for to whom):

Romans 15:21 GNT:
οις *to whom* ουκ *it was not* ανηγγέλη *announced* περί *concerning* αυτού *him*, ὄψονται *they shall see;* και *and* οι [the] *ones who* ουκ ακηκόασι *heard not* συνήσουσι *shall perceive.*

He has his eyes on Spain (vs. 24 and 28). Some commentators think he never made it. It is believed he dies after the great conflagration in Rome July 64 AD.

Conclusion

The emphasis in this study has been to concentrate on the Apostle Paul's use of the Old Testament in the Roman Epistle. Acceptance of the authority of the Word of God is unquestioned. Paul's approach to the Old Testament is the same. He is a spiritual man as his writing indicates being an instrument of the Spirit of God in the process of inscripturation.

1 Corinthians 3:10:
According to the grace of God which was given to me, like a wise master builder (ἀρχιτέκτων, architektoôn, a chief constructor, architect or master builder) I laid a foundation, and another is building on it. But each man must be careful how he builds on it.

The commonly accepted definition for the Greek word θεόπνευστος, (theopneustos) is:

INSPIRATION—Meaning literally "God-breathed" (from 2 Tim. 3:16), and referring to the divinely authoritative writings of Holy Scripture, which God produced without destroying the individual styles of the writers.[145]

Paul cites the Old Testament 58 times in Romans. (Appendix III). The most of any of his writings. He mainly uses the LXX, then the Masoretic Text and one citation from the Targum (Aramaic translation of the Hebrew Bible), when citing Deuteronomy 30:12-14 at Romans 10:6-8. He used the LXX

---

145 Norman L. Geisler, and William E. Nix, A General Introduction to the Bible, Moody press, Chicago, 1976, page 452. cf. 2 Peter 1:20-21, conveyance God's revelation to men.

because the world's commerce had become Greek speaking. The New Testament was written in Koine Greek because it was the most widespread business language of the day. Rome also was the largest city of the world and would have a large Greek speaking Jewish population.

J. Gresham Machen emphasizes the proliferation of the use of Greek and the Roman empire's transition from Latin to Greek:

Thus in the first century after Christ Greek had become a world language. ... It is not surprising that Paul's letter to the Roman Church is written not in Latin but in Greek.[146]

Paul's extensive training and background as a Rabbi (Romans 11:1; Philippians 3:5) enabled him to grasp the meaning of the passages he cited. The Scriptures are spiritual words, so his citations of the Old Testament and their meaning are secured in the New Testament as God's Word.

---

146 J. Gresham Machen, New Testament Greek for Beginners. The Macmillan Company. Toronto, Canada, 1923, page 2.

Appendix I Outline: Paul's Epistle To The Romans

I. Introduction — 1:1-18

  A. The object of Paul's gospel — 1:1-8
    1. relationship of Paul to the gospel — 1:1
    2. revelation of Christ in the gospel — 1:2-5
    3. recipients of the gospel — 1:6-7
    4. salutation to the church at Rome, and his commendation of their faith — 1:8

  B. The Importance Of Paul's gospel — 1:9-18
    1. because of Paul's urgency to preach the gospel — 1:9-15
    2. because it is the power of God — 1:16
    3. because it reveals the righteousness of God the prophecy of Habakkuk — 1:17
    4. because it saves from the wrath of God — 1:18

II. Righteousness Of God In Salvation (Doctrine Of Salvation) — 1:19-8:39

  A. Need Of Righteousness Of God (Doctrine Of Condemnation) — 1:18-3:20

    1. condemnation of heathen — 1:18-32
      a. sin of heathen — 1:18-23,25
      b. judgment of heathen — 1:24,26-32
    2. condemnation of Jews — 2:1-3:8
      a. principles of judgment — 2:1-16
      b. historic failure of Jews — 2:17-29
      c. answers to the Jews — 3:1-8
    3. condemnation of all men — 3:9-20
      a. sin is universal — 3:9-12
      b. sin is pervasive — 3:13-18
        (1) demonstrated through speech — 3:13-14
        (2) demonstration through deeds — 3:15-17
        (3) demonstration through mindset — 3:18
      c. sin is conclusive — 3:19-20
        (1) all accountable — 3:19
        (2) no flesh justified — 3:20

  B. Provision Of Righteousness Of God

(Doctrine Of Justification)	3:21-5:21

1. manifestation of justification in Christ — 3:21-31
   a. apart from the law — 3:21
   b. through faith in Christ — 3:22a
   c. for all men — 3:22b-23
   d. because of Christ's death — 3:24-26
      (1) redemption for sinners — 3:24
      (2) propitiation of God — 3:25a
      (3) vindication of God — 3:25b-26
   e. it excludes pride in ourselves — 3:27-28
   f. it excludes prejudice towards others — 3:29-30
   g. it excludes presumption towards the law — 3:31
2. Illustration of justification from Old Testament — 4:1-25
   a. justification is only by faith by example of Abraham — 4:1-5
   b. justification is only by faith by example of King David — 4:6-8
   c. justification is not dependent on the rite of circumcision or is independent of external conditions — 4:9-12
   d. justification is through the righteousness of faith — 4:13-15
   e. prophecy concerning Abraham's descendants — 4:16-22
      (1) his faith corresponds to the promise of God — 4:18
      (2) his faith extends to the improbable — 4:19
      (3) his faith created confidence — 4:20
      (4) his faith motivated to action — 4:21
      (5) his faith is rewarded by grace — 4:22
   f. Abraham's justification account remains to benefit us — 4:23-25
      (1) faith in a resurrecting God — 4:23-24a
      (2) faith in a resurrected Lord — 4:24b
      (3) faith in a substitutionary savior — 4:25
3. Benefits of justification — 5:1-21
   a. to individuals — 5:1-11
      (1) justification gives us peace with God — 5:1
      (2) justification gives us confidence — 5:2a
      (3) justification gives us hope — 5:2b
      (4) justification gives us a triumphant attitude — 5:3-5

i. in joy of triumph	5:3a
ii. in knowledge of triumph	5:3a-4
iii. in assurance of triumph	5:5
(5) justification demonstrates God's redemptive love	5:6-8
i. it is unearned	5:6a
ii. it is sacrificial	5:6b
iii. it is unequaled	5:7-8
(6) justification is based on Christ's work	5:9-11
i. it is based on his violent death	5:9
ii. it completed when we were his enemies	5:10
iii. it is the only basis of reconciliation toward God	5:11
b. to race	5:12-21
(1) 2 men influence the whole human race	5:12-14
(2) 2 classifications apply to the whole race	5:15-16
i. difference in the character of the 2 acts	5:15
ii. difference in the circumstances of the 2 acts	5:16
iii. difference in the consequences of the 2 acts	5:17
(3) summary of the gifts of grace	5:18-21
i. life instead of death	5:18
ii. justification instead of judgment	5:19
iii. abundant grace instead of increased sin	5:20-21

C. Transforming Power Of Righteousness Of God
(Doctrine Of Sanctification/The Moral Results Of Justification)   6:1-8:39

1. Believer's position in regards to sin	6:1-23
a. the first question and its answer	6:1-14
(1) union with Christ means death to sin	6:2-4a
(2) union with Christ means participation in new life	6:4b-11
(3) union with Christ is incongruous with a life of sin	6:12-14
b. The second question and its answer	6:15-23
(1) there is no service of 2 masters	6:16-18
(2) there is no gain serving sin and death	6:19-21
(3) serving God yields eternal life and sanctification	6:22-23
2. Believer's practice in regards to the law	7:1-25
a. believer is free from the law	7:1-6
(1) question	

(2) illustration	7:1
(3) application	7:2-3
b. Believer's pre-conversion experience	7:4-6
(1) law reveals sin and makes sin alive	7:7-13
(2) sin kills	7:7-8
(3) sin deceives and kills	7:9-10
(4) law remains holy sin proliferates due to law	7:11
c. Believer's post-conversion experience	7:12-13
(1) recognition of the conflict	7:14-25
(2) reality of renewal of the will	7:14-17
(3) reality of the struggle with flesh	7:18-20
(4) conclusion	7:21-23
3. Believer's prospect in regards to the Spirit and victory over sin through the Holy Spirit according to the purpose and action of God	7:24-25
a. life in the Spirit means practical righteousness	8:1-39
(1) by restoration to holiness by the Spirit	8:1-11
(2) by the destruction of sin by the Spirit	8:1-4
(3) by destruction of death by the Spirit	8:5-9
b. life in the Spirit means confidence	8:10-11
(1) by final destination according to the Spirit	8:12-17
(2) by adoption according to the Spirit	8:12-13
(3) by assurance given by the Spirit	8:14-15
c. life in the Spirit means final regeneration	8:15-17
(1) future glory outweighs present sufferings	8:18-25
(2) creation is joined to this event	8:18
(3) first fruits of the Spirit is a guarantee	8:19-22
d. life in the Spirit means intercession for us	8:23-25
e. life in the Spirit reveals God's redemptive purpose	8:26-27
(1) divine plan is revealed in our salvation	8:28-39
(2) divine plan excludes failure	8:28-30
i. permanence of God's love covers every circumstance	8:31-37
ii. what right do you have to God's pardon?	8:31-32
ii. who owns the right to condemnation?	8:33
f. will the efforts of brute force nullify the plan of God	8:34
g. divine plan excludes separation from God	8:35-37
	8:38-39
III. Righteousness Of God In History (the Problem Of Jewish Unbelief And Its Future Reversal)	
	9:1-11:36

A. Paul's burden and distress over Israel's unbelief
   1. intensity of his grief   9:1-5
   2. spiritual tragedy of Israel   9:1-3
                                                                            9:4-5

B. Election Of Israel
   (Vindication Of God's Righteousness With Israel)
                                                                            9:6-33
   1. election as explanation of Israel's unbelief
     a. not all are Israel from Israel,   9:6-13
        there are 2 Israels
     b. lineal corporeal descent not the determiner   9:6
     c. children of promise are descendants   9:7
     d. the one who calls determines choice   9:8
        of descendants
   2. objections to God's election answered   9:9-13
     a. answer to unrighteousness in God   9:14-29
     b. answer to denial of human culpability   9:14-18
     c. Hosea's prophecy   9:19-24
     d. scriptural proof of election of remnant   9:25-26
     e. outcome of election results in belief   9:27-29
        (justification by faith) and unbelief
        (rejection of justification by faith)
        and Isaiah's prophecy
     f. Isaiah's prophecy   9:30-33
                                                                             9:33

C. Rejection Of Israel
   1. The failure of Israel   10:1-10:21
     a. salvation is not zeal without knowledge   10:1-4
     b. salvation is not self defined righteousness   10:1-2
     c. salvation is belief in Christ that ends this law   10:3
   2. The accessibility of the gospel Old Testament   10:4
       prophetic proof (Moses)
     a. righteousness based on law is   10:5-10
        inextricably obligatory
     b. righteousness based on faith is God's work   10:5
     c. righteousness based on faith is confessional   10:6-8
   3. The universality of the gospel   10:9-10
       Old Testament prophetic proof (Isaiah and Joel)
     a. righteousness based on faith is indemnified   10:11-15
        and universally available
     b. righteousness based on faith is a sanctioned and   10:11-13
        authorized proclamation
   4. The unbelief of Israel Old Testament; prophetic proof   10:14-15

      (Moses, David and Isaiah)

a. the gospel proclamation can be ignored	10:16-21
b. nevertheless the gospel proclamation is heard through the calling of the Gentiles	10:16-18
c. disobedience and obstinance come from ignoring	10:19-20
	10:21
D. Restoration Of Israel	
1. the present election	11:1-36
a. like the days of Elijah	11:1-10
b. remnant of Jews of Israel are saved presently	11:1-4
c. the chosen of Israel obtain righteousness the rest are hardened	11:5-6
2. The future restoration	11:7-10
3. the gentiles benefit by their rejection	11:11-32
a. belief is the basis that grafts Jew or Gentile to the natural olive tree	11:11-16
b. faith is a mystery	11:17-24
c. Israel's calling is irrevocable though temporarily suspended	11:25-27
4. doxology	11:28-32
	11:33-36
IV. Righteousness Of God In Believer's Lives (Doctrine Of Sanctification)	
	12:1-15:13
A. Dedication to God	
	12:1,2
B. Duty to believer's and all men	
1. proper use of gifts	12:3-21
2. law of Christ and Christian practice in persecution	12:3-9
	12:9-21
C. Duty to the state and fellow citizens	
1. duty to state and role of legitimate government	13:1-14
a. because government is ordained by God	13:1-7
b. because government punishes evil doers to maintain justice	13:1-2
c. because government protects the innocent citizens	13:3,4b
d. subjection is due to avoid penalty and be law abiding	13:4a
e. taxes and other civil obligations support legitimate government	13:5
2. duty to one's neighbor	13:6-7
	13:8-14

D. Duties to weak and strong Christians	14:1-15:13
1. be generous	14:1-12
2. build up one another	14:13-23
3. please others like Christ did	15:1-6
a. responsibility we have to please others	15:1-2
b. reason we should please others	15:3-5
c. result of pleasing others	15:6
4. consequences of the work of Christ accept others	15:7-13
V. Conclusion	15:14-16:27
A. Paul's rules in ministry	15:14-21
1. cause mature Christians to apply what they know	15:14-15
2. carry on ministry of presenting Gentiles to God	15:15-16
3. create new works	15:17-21
B. Paul's future plans create new works	15:22-33
C. Personal greetings and commendations	16:1-27

APPENDIX II   LXX TO MASORETIC TEXT PSALM NUMBERING:

PSALMS 1-8 ARE THE SAME IN HEBREW AND THE SEPTUAGINT.

PSALMS 9 AND 10 IN HEBREW ARE COMBINED AS PSALM 9 IN THE SEPTUAGINT.

PSALMS 11-113 IN HEBREW ARE PSALMS 10-112 IN THE SEPTUAGINT (HEBREW-1 = GREEK).

PSALMS 114 AND 115 IN HEBREW ARE COMBINED AS PSALM 113 IN THE SEPTUAGINT.

PSALM 116 IN HEBREW IS DIVIDED INTO PSALMS 114 AND 115 IN THE SEPTUAGINT.

PSALMS 117-146 IN HEBREW ARE PSALMS 116-145 IN THE SEPTUAGINT (HEBREW-1 = GREEK).

PSALM 147 IN HEBREW IS DIVIDED INTO PSALMS 146 AND 147 IN THE SEPTUAGINT.

PSALMS 148-150 ARE THE SAME IN HEBREW AND THE SEPTUAGINT.

Appendix III Cross reference

CODES
L1 FIRST USE OF THE LAW (CONDEMNATION)
L2 SECOND USE OF THE LAW (REMEDIATION)
L3 THIRD USE OF THE LAW (REGULATION)
H   CITING OLD TESTAMENT HISTORICAL RECORD TO DEMONSTRATE THE CHARACTER OF GOD AND CORROBORATE PAUL'S ASSERTIONS
P   PROPHETIC CONTEXT (FULFILLED, FULFILLING OR WILL BE FULFILLED)

CODE	Romans	Old Testament citation	introductory or confirmatory formula B-before A-after	
P	1:17	Habakkuk 2:4	καθὼς γέγραπται as it is has been written	B
L1L2 L3P	2:6	Psalm 62:12		
H	2:24	Isaiah 52:5; Ezekiel 36:20ff.	καθὼς γέγραπται as it is has been written	A
P	3:4	Psalm 51:4	καθὼς γέγραπται as it is has been written	B
L1	3:10-12	Psalm 14:1; 53:1-4	καθὼς γέγραπται ὅτι as it is has been written that	B
L1	3:13	Psalm 5:9; 140:3	inferred from 3:10	B
L1	3:14	Psalm 10:7	inferred from 3:10	B
L1	3:15-17	Isaiah 59:7	inferred from 3:10	B
L1	3:18	Psalm 36:1	inferred from 3:10	B
P	4:3	Genesis 15:6	τί γὰρ ἡ γραφὴ λέγει For what does the Scripture say?	B
L3	4:7-8	Psalm 32:1-2	καθάπερ καὶ Δαυὶδ λέγει just as David also speaks	B
L3	4:9	Genesis 15:6	λέγομεν γάρ for we say	B
P	4:17	Genesis 17:5	καθὼς γέγραπται ὅτι as it is written that	B

P	4:18	Genesis 15:5	εἰς τὸ γενέσθαι ... κατὰ τὸ εἰρημένον so that he might become...that which had been spoken	B
P	4:22	Genesis 15:6	διὸ therefore	B
L1L2 L3	7:7	Exodus 20:17; Deuteronomy 5:21	εἰ μὴ ὁ νόμος ἔλεγεν if the law had not said	B
PH	8:36	Psalm 44:22	καθὼς γέγραπται ὅτι as it is has been written that	B
P	9:7	Genesis 21:12	ἀλλ' but	B
P	9:9	Genesis 18:10	ἐπαγγελίας γὰρ ὁ λόγος οὗτος for this is the word of promise	B
P	9:12	Genesis 25:23	ἐρρέθη αὐτῇ it was said to her	B
PH	9:13	Malachi 1:2-3	καθὼς γέγραπται as it is has been written	B
PH	9:15	Exodus 33:19	τῷ Μωϋσεῖ γὰρ λέγει for he says to Moses	B
PH	9:17	Exodus 9:16	λέγει γὰρ ἡ γραφὴ τῷ Φαραὼ for the Scripture says to Pharaoh	B
PH	9:25	Hosea 2:23	ὡς καὶ ἐν τῷ Ὡσηὲ λέγει as also in Hosea He says	B
PH	9:26	Hosea 1:10	inferred from 9:25	B
PH	9:27	Isaiah 10:22; Genesis 22:17; Hosea 1:10	Ἡσαΐας δὲ κράζει ὑπὲρ τοῦ Ἰσραήλ Isaiah cries out concerning Israel	B
PH	9:28	Isaiah 10:23	inferred from 9:25	B
PH	9:29	Isaiah 1:9	καὶ καθὼς προείρηκεν Ἡσαΐας and as Isaiah foretold	B
PH	9:33	Isaiah 28:16; Isaiah 8:14	καθὼς γέγραπται as it is has been written	B
P	10:6	Deuteronomy	ἡ δὲ ἐκ πίστεως δικαιοσύνη	B

132

		30:12	οὕτως λέγει but the righteousness out of faith speaks this	
P	10:7	Deuteronomy 30:13	Same as 6 + ἤ,	B
P	10:8	Deuteronomy 30:14	ἀλλὰ τί λέγει but what does it say	B
P	10:11	Isaiah 28:16	λέγει γὰρ ἡ γραφή for the Scripture says	B
P	10:13	Joel 2:32	γάρ for	B
P	10:15	Isaiah 52:7	καθὼς γέγραπται as it is has been written	B
P	10:16	Isaiah 53:1	Ἡσαΐας γὰρ λέγει for Isaiah says	B
H	10:18	Psalm 19:4	ἀλλὰ λέγω but I say	B
P	10:19	Deuteronomy 32:21	ἀλλὰ λέγω but I say	B
P	10:20	Isaiah 65:1	σαΐας δὲ ἀποτολμᾷ καὶ λέγει but Isaiah is very bold and says	B
PH	10:21	Isaiah 65:2	πρὸς δὲ τὸν Ἰσραὴλ λέγει but for Israel he says	B
H	11:3	1 Kings 19:10	λέγει ἡ γραφή the Scripture says coupled with a question ἢ οὐκ οἴδατε ἐν Ἠλίᾳ Literally, 'Or not know you what the *Scripture says* in Elijah?'	B
H	11:4	1 Kings 19:18	τί λέγει αὐτῷ ὁ χρηματισμός ; but what says to him the divine answer	B
P	11:8	Deuteronomy 29:4; Isaiah 29:10	καθὼς γέγραπται as it is has been written	B
P	11:9-10	Psalm 69:22-23	καὶ Δαυὶδ λέγει and David says	B
P	11:26	Isaiah 59:20-21	καθὼς γέγραπται as it is has been written	B

P	11:27	Isaiah 27:9	inferred from 11:26	B
H	11:34	Isaiah 40:13	Ὦ βάθος Oh, the depth	B
H	11:35	Job 35:7; 41;11	inferred from 11:33	B
PL3	12:19	Proverbs 20:22	γέγραπται γάρ for it has been written λέγει κύριος Says the Lord	B
PL3	12:20	Proverbs 25:21-22	inferred from 12:19	B
L3	13:9	Exodus 20:13ff.; Leviticus19:18	τὸ γάρ for this, καὶ and	B
PL3	14:11	Isaiah 45:23	γέγραπται γάρ for it has been written	B
PL3	15:3	Psalm 69:9	ἀλλὰ καθὼς γέγραπται but as it has been written	B
PL3	15:9	Psalm 18:49 or 2 Samuel 22:50	καθὼς γέγραπται as it is has been written	B
PL3	15:10	Deuteronomy 32:43	καὶ πάλιν λέγει and again he says	B
PL3	15:11	Psalm 117:1	καὶ πάλιν and again	B
PL3	15:12	Isaiah 11:10	Καὶ πάλιν Ἡσαΐας λέγει and again Isaiah says	B
P	15:21	Isaiah 52:15	ἀλλὰ καθὼς γέγραπται but as it is has been written	B

Appendix IV   Abbreviations

AD (OR A.D.) IS AN ABBREVIATION FOR THE LATIN EXPRESSION "ANNO DOMINI", WHICH TRANSLATES TO "THE YEAR OF OUR LORD", AND EQUIVALENT TO C.E. (THE COMMON ERA)

CF. (CONFER) MEANS TO SEE A GIVEN CITATION FOR COMPARISON

E.G. (EXEMPLI GRATIA) MEANS "FOR EXAMPLE"

GNT   GREEK NEW TESTAMENT

I.E. (ID EST) MEANS "THAT IS" OR "IN OTHER WORDS"

IBID. (IBIDEM) MEANS "IN THE SAME PLACE" AND IS USED IN CITATIONS TO REFER TO A PREVIOUSLY LISTED WORK

LXX   SEPTUAGINT

MT   MASORETIC TEXT

VID. VIDETUR, A LATIN WORD MEANING "APPARENTLY" OR "SO IT APPEARS

VIZ. (VIDELICET) MEANS "NAMELY" OR "THAT IS TO SAY"

BIBLIOGRAPHY

Alford, Henry, Alford's Greek New Testament, Vol., II, Baker Book House, Grand Rapids, Michigan, reprinted, 1980.

Baker, Alvin, ThD, Systematic Theology, Lecture notes, 'The depravity of man', Northeastern Bible College, Fall 1981,

Baker, Alvin, L., ThD, Knowing the Will of God: Toward a Practical Theology, Part 1 and part 2 may be found here: www.logos.com Volume 8, Number 2, 1986 (part 1), Volume 8, Number 1, 1985, (part 2 conclusion) (PDF download on 4/12/2018).

Barnes, Albert, Barnes' Notes on the Bible, Volume 13 - Acts – Romans, Electronic Edition STEP Files AGES Software Rio, WI USA Version 1.0 © 2000.

Barnes, Albert, Barnes' Notes on the Old Testament, Deuteronomy. Electronic Edition STEP Files AGES Software Rio, WI USA Version 1.0 © 1999.

Behm, Johannes, ed. Gerhard Kittel, trans. Geoffrey Bromiley, (TDNT) Theological Dictionary of the New Testament Vol. I. Vol V, Wm. B. Eerdmans Publishing Grand Rapids, Michigan, reprinted 1979 10th printing 1979.

Berkhof, Louis, Systematic Theology, Wm. B. Eerdmans Publishing, Grand Rapids, Michigan, reprinted 1977.

Bennett, Robert H., I Am Not Afraid: Demon Possession And Spiritual Warfare, Concordia Publishing House, St Louis, Missouri, 2013.

Brenton, Sir Lancelot C. L., The Septuagint Version: Greek and English, Septuagint version of the Old Testament, Zondervan Corporation, Grand Rapids, Michigan, 1970.

Brown, Francis, with Driver, S. R., and Briggs, Charles A., trans., Edward Robinson, The New Brown Driver Briggs Gesenius Hebrew Aramaic English Lexicon, Associated Publishers and Authors, Inc., Lafayette, Indiana, 1980.

Bultmann, Rudolf, ed. Gerhard Kittel, trans. Geoffrey Bromiley, Theological Dictionary of the New Testament Vol. I, Wm. B. Eerdmans Publishing Grand Rapids, Michigan, reprinted 1979.

Burton, Ernest De Witt, Syntax Of The Moods And Tenses In New Testament Greek, The University of Chicago Press Chicago, Illinois, 1900.

Chafer, Lewis Sperry, Systematic Theology, Vol I; Vol II, Dallas Seminary Press, 1947.

Clarke Adam, Adam Clarke's Commentary on the New Testament, Electronic Edition STEP Files Copyright © 1999, Parsons Technology, Inc, section: .

Cranfield, C. E. B. Romans, A Shorter Commentary, Wm. B. Eerdmans Publishing Grand Rapids, Michigan, copyright T & T Clark, 1985.

Delitzsch, F., trans. Francis Bolton, Commentary on the Old Testament Vol. V, second section: Psalms, Wm. B. Eerdmans Publishing Grand Rapids, Michigan, reprinted 1979 second Volume.

Denney, James, D.D. ed., W. Robertson Nicoll, The Expositor's Greek Testament, Vol. II, Wm. B. Eerdmans Publishing Grand Rapids, Michigan, reprinted 1979.

Dillenberger, John ed., Sermon: Two kinds of Righteousness, Martin Luther Selections From His Writings, Anchor Books, Doubleday & Company, Inc, Garden City, New York, 1961.

Driver, S. R., A Critical and Exegetical Commentary on Deuteronomy, Charles Scribner and Sons, 1902.

Eadie, John, The John Eadie Greek Text Commentaries, The Ephesians, Baker Book house, Grand Rapids, Michigan, reprinted 1979, from T & T Clark 1883 edition.

Elliger, Karl, Rudolph ed., Wilhelm Biblia Hebraica Stuttgartensia, Deutsche Bibelstiftung, Stuttgart, Germany, 1967/77.

Fairbairn, Patrick. The Typology of Scripture, Zondervan Publishing House, Grand Rapids, Michigan, 1952,

Feinberg, Charles L., ed., R. Laird Harris, (TWOT) Theological Wordbook of the Old Testament, Vol 2, Moody Press, Chicago, 1980.

Friedrich, Gerhard, ed. Gerhard Kittel, trans. Geoffrey Bromiley, Theological Dictionary of the New Testament Vol. III, Wm. B. Eerdmans Publishing Grand Rapids, Michigan, reprinted 1979.

Foxe, John, B o o k s F o r T h e A g e s, AGES Software • Albany, OR USA, Hartland Publications • Rapidan, VA USA Version 1.0 © 1997.

Geisler, Norman L. and William E. Nix, A General Introduction to the Bible, Moody press, Chicago, 1979,

Godet, Frederic L, St Paul's Epistle to the Roman Theological Library. trans. A.Cusin, new series., Vol. I and II, Edinburgh: T & T Clark, 38 George Street. 1881.

Greenlee, J. Harold, A Concise Exegetical Grammar of New Testament Greek, Wm. B. Eerdmans Publishing Grand Rapids, Michigan, reprinted 1979.

Greeven, Heinrich ed. Gerhard Kittel, trans. Geoffrey Bromiley, (TDNT) Theological Dictionary of the New Testament Vol. III, Wm. B. Eerdmans Publishing Grand Rapids, Michigan, reprinted 1979 10th printing 1979.

Grounds, Vernon C., Baker's Dictionary of Theology, Everett Harrison, ed., Baker Book House, Grand Rapids, Michigan, 1978.

Grundmann, Walter, ed. Gerhard Kittel, trans. Geoffrey Bromiley, (TDNT) Theological Dictionary of the New Testament Vol. I, Wm. B. Eerdmans Publishing Grand Rapids, Michigan, reprinted 1979 10th printing 1979.

Haldane, Robert, Exposition of the Epistle to the Romans, with remarks on the Commentaries of Dr. Macknight, Professor Moses Stuart, and Professor Tholuck, New York: Robert carter, 58 Canal street,and Pittsburgh, 56 market street. 1847.

Hauck, Friedrich ed. Gerhard Kittel, trans. Geoffrey Bromiley, (TDNT) Theological Dictionary of the New Testament Vol. V, Wm. B. Eerdmans Publishing Grand Rapids, Michigan, reprinted 1979 10th printing 1979.

Hertz, Dr. J. H. C. H., ed.., late Chief Rabbi of the British Empire, The Pentateuch and Haftoahs, second edition, Socini Press, London, 1970.

Hodge, Charles, Commentary on the Epistle to the Romans, Philadelphia: Alfred Martien, 1214 Chestnut Street.1873.

Hodge, Caspar Wistar, gen. ed., James Orr, International Standard Bible Encyclopedia, Volume III, Wm. B. Eerdmans Publishing Grand Rapids, Michigan, reprinted 1978.

Hughes, Philip Edgcumbe, Baker's Dictionary of Theology, eds., Everett Harrison, Geoffrey Bromiley, Carl Henry, Baker Book House, Grand Rapids, Michigan, 1978.

Jepson, Alfred, eds., G. Johannes Botterweck, Helmer Ringgren, trans., John T. Willis, (TDOT) Theological Dictionary of the Old Testament, Vol I, Wm. B. Eerdmans Publishing Company, Grand Rapids, Michigan, 1974.

Keil, C.F. & Delitzsch F., trans. James Martin, Commentary on the Old Testament Vol I, V, X, Wm. B. Eerdmans Publishing Grand Rapids, Michigan, reprinted 1979-1982.

Kelly, William, Baker's Dictionary of Theology, Everett Harrison, ed., Baker Book House, Grand Rapids, Michigan, 1978.

Kruger, Michael, August 18, 2014 , 'You Don't Think Learning the Biblical Languages is Worth It? Think Again', retrieved from website November 27, 2020, www.michaeljkruger.com/you-dont-think-learning-the-biblical-languages-is-worth-it-think-again.

Lenski, R. C. H., Commentary on the New Testament, Hendrickson Publishing, second printing March 2001.

Luther, Martin, Luther's Works, Hilton C. Oswald ed., Vol. 25, Lectures On Romans, Concordia Publishing House, St Louis, Missouri, 1972.

Machen, J. Gresham, New Testament Greek for Beginners. The Macmillan Company. Toronto, Canada, 1923.

M'Caig, Archibald, gen. ed., James Orr, (ISBE) International Standard Bible Encyclopedia, Volume III, Wm. B. Wm. B. Eerdmans Publishing, Grand Rapids, Michigan, reprinted 1978.

Meyer, H. A. W., Meyer's Critical and Exegetical Commentary on the New Testament, Romans, Vol. V., Alpha Greek Library, Winona Lake Wisconsin, reprinted 1980.

Mosiman, S. K., gen. ed., James Orr, International Standard Bible Encyclopedia, Volume I, Wm. B. Eerdmans Publishing Grand Rapids, Michigan, reprinted 1978.

Moule, H. C. G., Studies in Romans, Kregel Publications, Grand Rapids, Michigan, reprinted 1982 of 1892 edition, The Epistle of Paul The Apostle to the Romans. Cambridge University Press, London.

Packer, James I., ed. E. F. Harrison, Baker's Dictionary of Theology, Baker Book House, Grand Rapids, Michigan, 1978.

Payne, J. Barton, The Theology of the Older Testament, Zondervan publishing House, Grand rapids, Michigan, 1962, 11th printing 1978.

"Persecution of Christians", *Wikipedia*, Wikimedia Foundation, last edited on 13 June 2020.

Rienecker, Fritz, trans., Cleon L. Rogers Jr., Cleon Rogers III, A Linguistic Key to the Greek New Testament Vol 2., Zondervan Publishing House, 1980.

Renwick, Alexander M., Baker's Dictionary of Theology, Everett Harrison, ed., Baker Book House, Grand Rapids, Michigan, 1978.

Robertson, Archibald Thomas, Word Pictures in the New Testament, Vol. IV, The Epistles of Paul, Baker Book House, Grand Rapids, Michigan, 1931.

Rogers Cleon Jr., Rogers Cleon III, A Linguistic Key and Exegetical Key to the Greek New Testament, Zondervan Publishing House, 1998.

Sanday, W., Headlam, A. C., The International Critical Commentary Critical and Exegetical Commentary on the Epistle to the Romans, Edinburgh: T & T Clark, 1902.

Scaer, David, "Third Use of the Law: Resolving The Tension", 28th Annual Symposium on the Lutheran Confessions, Concordia Theological Seminary, January 2005, David P. Scaer, (PDF download on 2/02/2009).

Schaff, Philip History of the Christian Church, Charles Scribner's Sons, New York, Vol I, 1889.

Schmidt, W. H., eds., G. Johannes Botterweck, Helmer Ringgren, trans., John T. Willis, (TDOT) Theological Dictionary of the Old Testament, Vol III, Wm. B. Eerdmans Publishing Company, Grand Rapids, Michigan, 1974.

Schrenk, Gottlob, ed. Gerhard Kittel, trans. Geoffrey Bromiley, (TDNT) Theological Dictionary of the New

Testament Vol. I, Wm. B. Eerdmans Publishing Grand Rapids, Michigan, reprinted 1979, 10th printing 1979.

Sprinkle, Joe M. Baker Theological Dictionary of the Bible, ed. Walter A. Elwell, Baker Books, Grand Rapids, Michigan, 1996.

Stahlin, Gustav ed. Gerhard Kittel, trans. Geoffrey Bromiley, (TDNT) Theological Dictionary of the New Testament Vol. VII, Wm. B. Eerdmans Publishing Grand Rapids, Michigan, reprinted 1979 10th printing 1979.

Strong, James, Parsons Technology, Inc. Cedar Rapids, Iowa, electronic edition step files copyright © 1998.

Thayer, Joseph Henry, translated revised and enlarged, Greek English-Lexicon of the New Testament, Harper & Brothers, New York, Cincinnati, Chicago, American Book Company, 1889.

Tchividjian, William Graham Tullian, excerpts from 'Theology of Glory vs. Theology of the Cross'. The Christian Post, July 12, 2012, retrieved from website, www.christianpost.com/news/theology-of-glory-vs-theology-of-the-cross.html (HTML download on 2/18/2021)

The Formula of Concord, Concordia Publishing House 2005, (Epitome VI, 1).

(TDNTA) Theological Dictionary of the New Testament Abridged, ed., Gerhard Kittel and Gerhard Friedrich trans., Geoffrey W. Bromiley, Abridged in One Volume, 1985.

Vincent, Marvin R., Vincent's Word Studies, Vol. 2, The Writings of John: The Gospel, The Epistles, The Apocalypse, Vol. 3 The Epistles of Paul: Romans, Corinthians, Ephesians,

Philippians, Colossians, Philemon, Parsons Technology, Inc. Hiawatha, Iowa, electronic edition step files copyright © 1998.

Vine, W.E. Expository Dictionary of New Testament Words, Fleming H. Revell Company, Old Tappan, New Jersey, reprinted 1966.

Walker, W. L., gen. ed., James Orr, International Standard Bible Encyclopedia, Volume V, Wm. B. Eerdmans Publishing Grand Rapids, Michigan, reprinted 1978.

White, William ed., R. Laird Harris, (TWOT) Theological Wordbook of the Old Testament, Vol 2, Moody Press, Chicago, 1980.

www.ingramcontent.com/pod-product-compliance
Lightning Source LLC
Chambersburg PA
CBHW061655040426
42446CB00010B/1749